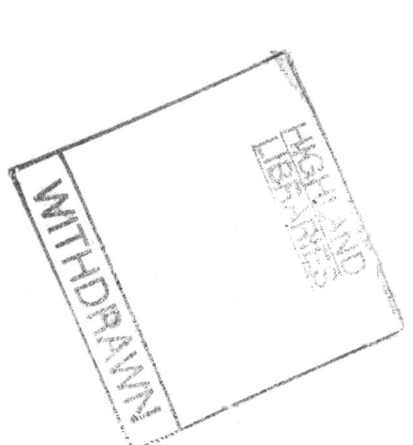

ODETTE

WORLD WAR TWO'S DARLING SPY

PENNY STARNS

The History Press

Dedicated to all the brave women
who served in the SOE

First published 2009
This paperback edition first published 2018

The History Press
The Mill, Brimscombe Port
Stroud, Gloucestershire, GL5 2QG
www.thehistorypress.co.uk

British Library Cataloguing in Publication Data.
A catalogue record for this book is available from the British
Library.

ISBN 978 0 7509 8437 9

Typesetting and origination by The History Press
Printed and bound by CPI Group (UK) Ltd

CONTENTS

Acknowledgements 7

Introduction 8

1. Childhood Years 13
2. Adopting England 24
3. Baker Street Specials 35
4. Becoming a Spy 46
5. Operation Clothier 59
6. Cannes and the Spindle Network 70
7. Marseille 80
8. Radio Days 89
9. Betrayal 100
10. Interrogations 110
11. Ravensbrück 126
12. Liberty 138
13. Counting the Cost 149
14. Darling of the Press 159
15. SOE Undermined 170

16. Fallen Heroine   180

17. The Ward Vendetta   190

18. The Official Line   200

19. The Apology   212

20. Reflections   226

Appendix 1: Awarding of the George Cross   235

Appendix 2: Recommendation for MBE   237

Appendix 3: Chronology of Events   238

Index   246

ACKNOWLEDGEMENTS

The most important person to acknowledge for his contribution to this book is my friend Dr Luc Berlivet. He has generously assisted me every step of the way, by translating French primary sources into English, and by providing me with a French perspective on historical events. I therefore extend a heartfelt thank you to Luc. I am grateful to all the archivists at The National Archives and Imperial War Museum who have facilitated my research. Moreover, Linda Morgan at the Special Forces Club, and Squadron Leader Bob Naeem of 282 ATC Squadron Royal Air Force, kindly provided me with valuable assistance.

Special thanks are due to Dr Maurizio Marinelli, Jo Denman and Derrick Shaw for their practical support and encouragement. In addition, there are many others who have actively supported the writing process by listening to my ideas and giving me valuable feedback, these include: Elizabeth Goulding, Jo Foster and Brenda Wood. In this respect I am also greatly indebted to my editor Sophie Bradshaw.

Finally I would like to say thank you to James and Zoe, Michael and Rocha, Lewis and Rosie, Zakary, Charlie, Logan and Daisy, and Edward Starns for providing me with love and humour.

INTRODUCTION

With the outbreak of the Second World War in 1939 many European women embraced the opportunity to support their individual countries in their time of desperate need. Those who were fit and able took over the industrial and agricultural work that was traditionally seen as a male domain. Others worked on the front line as military nurses or in the transport sections of the fighting forces. Yet another, smaller and more select group of women actually worked behind enemy lines. These special services women were trained as secret agents and established underground Resistance movements across Europe. They provided such movements with crucial intelligence information, dynamite and armaments, radio equipment, secret hideaways, food and clothing. They guided Allied bombers into enemy-occupied territories, led raids on Gestapo headquarters and sabotaged rail and communication networks. They were in essence a vital, and for the most part secret, component of the war effort.

This book tells the story of one such woman, an incredible and courageous individual who became the first woman to receive both the British George Cross and the French *Chevalier de la Légion d'honneur* for her courage in the face of the enemy. Born in Amiens as Odette Marie Celine Brailly she assumed a variety of names during the course of her war service. Yet she was universally known to both the British and French public in the post-war years simply as Odette. At a time when it was rare for a woman to step out of the domestic environment, let alone engage in dangerous undercover war work, Odette had entered the brink of hell and survived against the odds to testify against her persecutors at the International Nazi War Crimes Tribunals in Hamburg. Her contribution to the war effort was deemed to be all the more remarkable because she was the mother of three small daughters.

Odette was a member of the Special Operations Executive (SOE), a British secret service organisation that was established to encourage underground covert resistance within enemy-occupied territories, and to gain vital information to assist the war effort. In the spring of 1943, while she was engaged in dangerous espionage work in Nazi-occupied France, Odette was arrested along with her supervisor, Captain Peter Churchill. En route to Fresnes prison she managed to convince her captors that she was married to her supervisor and that he was, in fact, closely related to the British Prime Minister Winston Churchill. In total, Odette was subjected to fourteen Gestapo interrogations and brutal torture. All her toenails were pulled out and her back was scorched with red hot irons; yet she clung rigidly to her fabricated story about her supervisor, and also refused to disclose the whereabouts of another British agent and a radio officer. Significantly for the intelligence service, she succeeded in deflecting attention away from her 'husband' by claiming that he was only in France at her request, and knew nothing of her activities with the French Resistance. Nevertheless, her refusal to co-operate with her captors had severe consequences, and Odette was subsequently condemned to death on two counts by a Gestapo court at Avenue Foch. However, on hearing this news, she had simply replied politely:'Then you will have to make up your mind on which count I am to be executed, because I can only die once!'

Incensed Gestapo officers quickly responded to her insolence by transferring Odette from Fresnes prison in Paris to the notorious Ravensbrück concentration camp. Here Odette was kept in solitary confinement as a political prisoner to await her execution. Within the walls of this all-female camp the SS women guards ruled supreme. Each day and night they patrolled the confines of the camp with their vicious dogs and inflicted cruel and sadistic treatment on their despairing prisoners. It was during this nightmare period that Odette became fully aware of the horrors of the Holocaust and other Nazi atrocities.

Miraculously Odette survived her internment at Ravensbrück, and in 1946 she received her honours from Britain and France. They were, she insisted, accepted on behalf of all the gallant women who had worked within the Special Operations Executive. But despite her own deep sense of humility, Odette became a celebrated heroine on both sides of the Channel. Furthermore, a major film about her war time exploits, starring Dame Anna Neagle, was released in 1950. Thus for a considerable time, Odette remained the darling of the British popular press. But the story of Odette is not without controversy. During the post-war years there were several officials who disbelieved her recollection of events and others who cast doubt on her personal and professional integrity. There were even some who fervently believed that she did not deserve to be the first woman to receive the George Cross medal. Subsequently, the organisation and administration of the SOE was also subjected to increased scrutiny and criticism, and a negative wave of publicity threatened to destroy Odette's peace of mind along with her gallant reputation. But the prolonged media attention and controversy made her even more determined to defend not only her own honour, but also that of her comrades, since the role of women in war was deliberately downplayed by many who supported the notion of a patriarchal society in the post-war years. At times it appeared that Odette was on a one-woman mission to emphasise the role of female SOE agents, and to ensure that these women and their brave sacrifices were respectfully remembered

This book, therefore, highlights not only the danger and excitement of espionage work, along with the determination of all those who were involved with Resistance work, but also the warmth, generosity, intelligence and sense of humour of its heroine. Ultimately, the story of Odette demonstrates the enduring, eternal and uplifting nature of the human spirit. Ten years before her death in 1995, she stressed once more that most of the women who suffered profoundly at the hands of the Gestapo did not survive to tell their own stories. She strongly believed that her own personal experiences should be recorded for future generations. The memory of Odette's fallen comrades remained with her throughout her life, and she stated categorically on numerous occasions that: 'My story is also their story.' It is hoped that through the pages of this book Odette's experiences will, to some extent, illuminate the lives of the comrades she never forgot. Furthermore, as far as possible, Odette's moving and memorable story is told in her own words using extracts from her oral history testimonies and personnel files. The riveting story of Odette is primarily an account of dangerous political intrigue in Nazi-occupied France, intertwined with the fascinating personal experiences of an extraordinarily determined and courageous young woman.

Sources

The primary research material for this book consists mainly of Odette's oral history testimonies and her recently opened Special Operations Executive personnel files. (These files were opened in 2004 and can be found at The National Archives in Richmond, London.) This material is supplemented with other primary source documents that have been obtained in Britain and France. J. Tickell's fictionalised biography of Odette should also be mentioned. It was published as *Odette: the Story of a British Spy* in 1949.

I

CHILDHOOD YEARS

Europe during the late nineteenth century was character-
ised by rapid industrialisation, wars of unification, a quest
for colonial expansion, newly emerging ideologies such
as nationalism and socialism, and a steadily increasing
population. Epidemics were rife, and scientific discoveries
and Darwin's theory of evolution had prompted an almost
obsessive preoccupation with the health and fitness of
individual nations. Due to a fundamental misapplication
of evolutionary theory, colonial conquest, wars and disease
were all viewed as part of an essential global struggle that
ensured the survival of the strongest of human races. Some
scientists even believed that wars were vital because they
supposedly acted as a purification process that eliminated
inferior beings. By the turn of the century, nationalism
had usurped both liberalism and socialism to become the
dominant ideology across the continent, and nations forged
a system of alliances in preparation for war. The German
economy grew rapidly stronger, and fuelled by intense waves
of nationalism the Kaiser embarked on a policy of Welpolitik
in order to gain colonies for his country. An Anglo-German
naval arms race began, and France became England's closest
political ally. Events in Russia and Serbia also contributed to

the increasing tension. Thus, by the time Odette Marie Celine Brailly made her entry into the world, in Amiens on 28 April 1912, a tumultuous Europe was already preparing for a major conflict. Her father Gaston Brailly had been secretly wishing for a son, but he quickly became besotted with his first-born child. Odette resembled her mother Yvonne, and was a very attractive baby, with deep brown eyes and fine curly hair. Gaston did not have to wait long for his secret wish to be granted, as Odette's brother Louis was born barely a year later.

The siblings were emotionally very close, despite the fact that their temperaments were as different as chalk and cheese. They were also reasonably obedient children, perhaps because the whole family were strict Catholics. Their mother Yvonne was a young, slender, petite woman with deep-set brown eyes and angular features. By nature she was reserved and painfully shy. In contrast, their father Gaston was, by all accounts, a proud, intelligent but volatile man with a finely tuned sense of justice. He had worked tirelessly in a tedious but secure position in a local bank until the First World War broke out in 1914. Then, like many of his fellow countrymen, he volunteered for military service. His innate intelligence and character ensured that he was often extremely critical of his superior officers, and of French military strategy. Consequently his commanders regarded him as subversive and potentially mutinous. Although his superiors in the 52nd Regiment of Infantry undoubtedly regarded him as a disruptive influence, his military career was littered with numerous exploits of extreme courage. Indeed, Sergeant Gaston Brailly died a hero. During the battle of Verdun two of his soldiers went missing; refusing to continue to a safe position without them, he went back to the front line. He eventually discovered them lying in agony, groaning from the pain that had been inflicted upon them by their severe wounds.

But, as he attempted to drag the men back to the safety of their platoon, they received a direct hit from a shell that claimed the lives of all three. Gaston was killed just thirty days before the Armistice of 11 November 1918, and was duly awarded the *Croix de Guerre* and the *Médaille Militaire* for his courage on the field of battle. His young wife Yvonne was left to bring up Odette and Louis alone.

Lest they forget their father and his sense of heroic duty to France and his comrades, both children were taken to Gaston's graveside in La Madeline cemetery every Sunday by their paternal grandparents. Neither of the latter believed that the Armistice marked the end of a war to end all wars. In fact, both of these staunch Picardy folk firmly expected the Germans to initiate another world war during their lifetimes, despite political optimism to the contrary and the presence of a newly formed League of Nations. They constantly reminded their grandchildren of the handsome, eager French soldiers who had departed for war full of youth and vigour, only to be returned to their homes dismembered, disfigured and disillusioned. Too many fathers, sons, husbands and brothers had been taken to early graves by the prolonged and utterly miserable conflict. Others, they said, were physically, emotionally and psychologically damaged beyond repair; men whose permanent, silent and catatonic expressions were only broken by intermittent screams of terror as they were momentarily transported to the horrors of the battlefield. Those who were not obviously suffering from shell shock or dismemberment often bore the deep but invisible scars of chemical warfare. These unseen lesions on the lungs killed them slowly and painfully, a long time after the hostilities of the First World War had ceased. As Odette recalled, she and her brother were never allowed to forget these men who had given so much for France and the world.

My family had always lived on the battlefields of war. I was brought up with the image of my father who had been a very brave man. Every Sunday after church I was taken with my brother to his grave. My grandfather used to say, 'in another twenty years there will be another war and it will be your duty, both of you, to do as well as your father did.' Of course, I listened to this for years. I was always brought up with a sense of duty. I was not war minded, but the seed was there, that like my father, when the time came, I had to do what I could.[1]

On Christmas Day 1918 a picture of Gaston smiling in his full military regalia was positioned in pride of place on the living-room mantlepiece. Festivities were quiet and reflective with occasional outbursts of tears from the subdued women and bewildered children. But with a fixed determination and a good deal of stoical inner strength it was Grandfather Brailly who successfully rallied the family to focus on the future. He had never been inclined towards the destructive emotion of self-pity and firmly believed that there was probably some rhyme or reason behind whatever life threw at him. Perhaps, he reasoned to himself in his more thoughtful moments, these challenging life events were dictated by a greater being for the education of the soul. His Catholic upbringing strongly supported this view and he saw no reason to argue with the wisdom of God. He was a meticulously clean, tall and upright gentleman of impeccable manners and kindly disposition – though he did not suffer fools gladly, and always gave the appearance of an overly strict patriarch whose authority could not be questioned. He had a fashionable well-trimmed moustache, sturdy figure, kind deep brown eyes and a sprinkling of grey hair, and he hid his sorrow well. There was no doubt in his mind that God or fate had dealt him a severe blow. But he consoled himself continually with the thought that his son was a national hero. He had died honourably trying to save the lives of others. During the wet, blustery Amiens winters, when the family huddled around the warmth of a roaring fire, he would embrace and patiently reassure his grieving wife of this fact. As the months passed and the initial pain of his loss was dulled he took quiet delight in noticing the same lopsided smile of his son flickering across the face of Odette. Then he marvelled that the serious expression and frown lines he remembered so well from the heated political discussions he had shared with Gaston were clearly visible across the furrowed brow of young Louis. There were times when his son seemed almost palpable in the idiosyncrasies of his offspring. However, both children differed dramatically in their looks and temperament.

Louis was strong, lively, outgoing and energetic, whereas Odette was an introverted, temperamental and somewhat sickly child. The moment any virus inhabited her body it seemed to stay for the duration and inflict maximum damage upon her small physique. But at least the family had managed to survive the devastating 1918 influenza pandemic that had claimed the lives of 25 million people across Europe. Throughout her childhood, Odette's immune system was considered to be weak. Indeed, many of her earlier days were spent looking out of her bedroom window from her sickbed. In addition to fighting a seemingly continual flood of minor illnesses, Odette contracted poliomyelitis at the age of seven. This condition left her totally blind for three and a half years and paralysed for over a year. Speaking of this difficult period Odette credited her grandfather for cultivating her strength of mind.

I had a wonderful grandfather who did not suffer weaklings very easily. One had to learn to endure pain and suffering.

Even when I was blind he was absolutely marvellous and would never accept that I could not be as clever and as good at everything as I could be.[2]

There was no doubt that during her prolonged periods of illness and distress Odette's grandfather was a rock of dependability. He studiously ignored her stubborn sullenness and frequent outbursts of rage because he knew that they were born of childish frustration and despair. He patiently coaxed her to play the piano and fostered her love of Chopin and Mozart. He was extremely tough with her, instantly squashing the seemingly inevitable sense of gloom and self-pity that reared its ugly head from time to time. Her grandmother was equally firm, and insisted on teaching her granddaughter to bake bread and clean the house like any other Picardy girl. Between them they encouraged her strong wilful nature, believing that her stubbornness and volatile outbursts would, in some way, offset the restrictions of her sickly physical disposition. They had also, perhaps unwittingly, nurtured Odette's own indomitable and steely determination to overcome adversity.

In the meantime, Odette's mother Yvonne diligently traipsed the streets of Amiens in the hope of finding a medical specialist and a cure for her daughter's blindness. Just when all hope seemed to be lost, an unlikely cure emerged as a result of a visit to an aged and eccentric local herbalist. Yvonne was highly dubious of the man's credentials, dressed as he was in old, grimy clothes, and displaying an unnerving habit of talking quietly and quickly to himself as he brewed his foul-smelling concoctions. He lived in a narrow back street and his standard of hygiene left a lot to be desired. Apparently, even his neighbours gave him a very wide berth when they saw him out shopping for his potions or wandering around in the woods and fields collecting his herbs. His constant muttering both alarmed and disturbed them. But Yvonne was ready to try anything by this stage.

Over the previous three years she had already paid numerous, but quite useless, visits to spanking clean medical clinics with their neatly laid-out modern equipment. They had all been inhabited by doctors with clear credentials who had displayed long arrays of letters after their names; yet with all their combined medical knowledge they had not been able to devise a cure. Thus, with a growing sense of desperation she had found herself at her wits' end and reluctantly placing her faith in a muttering old man. But once he had peered and prodded Odette several times and asked Yvonne numerous questions, he had triumphantly produced a bottle of opaque liquid. He then proceeded to issue a set of strict instructions as to the application of his 'medicine' and a stern warning not to let the light back into Odette's eyes too quickly. Yvonne had politely expressed her thanks for the consultation and had paid the man a few francs. In truth, she had very little faith in the miniature bottle of liquid she had wrapped in a handkerchief and placed in her small brown bag. There was considerable surprise and joy in the Brailly household therefore, when only two weeks after this consultation Odette was able to make out the outlines of faces and furniture. Gradually, over the following weeks and months, her sight improved. Two years later her visual clarity was restored.

Odette recounted this story of her childhood battle with poliomyelitis and blindness as accurately as she could; but it is possible that her sight may have returned without the help of the backstreet herbalist. Poliomyelitis often produced encephalopathy, which could be accompanied by blindness. Once the poliomyelitis virus had run its course the swelling in the brain eventually subsided and sight was sometimes restored. Odette's herbal treatment may simply have coincided with the time at which the swelling in her brain was subsiding naturally. Nevertheless, her 'miracle cure' resulted in an unshakeable faith in the elderly herbalist, who was successfully consulted once again some time later when Odette contracted rheumatic fever. This particular illness confined her to bed for the whole of one summer and left her extremely weak. The herbalist was able to effect a dramatic improvement in her condition by teaching her special exercises for her joints and administering a mixture of foul-smelling potions. At this point in her life her brother Louis was dispatched to school in Lycée, and, at the end of the summer when she had recovered from rheumatic fever, Odette was sent to the convent of St Thérèse.

Odette's sickly disposition was often a topic of family discussion, and the elders in the Brailly family believed the stronger air of Normandy would in some way strengthen her health and nurture her in a way that the damp climate of Amiens could not. Yvonne was inclined to agree, and in 1925 she settled in a house in Saint Sens and a year later moved to Boulogne. By the time she was fourteen, therefore, Odette was living in Boulogne with her mother. Her face and body had gained some much-needed weight and her health had indeed improved. Louis remained in school in Lycée but joined them for holidays. The siblings spent their vacation periods rock climbing, exploring the rugged coastline and watching the English tripper ships travel to and fro across the Channel.

As young children they had gradually developed affection for the English. During the First World War their home had often been occupied by wounded English soldiers. Most of these had been nursed back to health by their mother and grandmother. Odette and Louis remembered vividly that when these soldiers were fully recovered, they would bounce them on their knees, laugh and play with them. Odette in particular loved their impeccable manners and soft spoken voices.

During their summers in Boulogne brother and sister would mimic the English accents, laugh at their clothes and discuss English and French history. The siblings always remained close but Odette developed an increasing desire for solitude as she grew older. Subsequently, she began to wander the cliffs of Normandy alone and immerse herself in the peace and tranquillity of the coastal countryside. Perhaps because of her previous years of enforced blindness, changing seasons were noted with relish and keen observation. No tree in blossom, budding flower or blade of grass escaped her fond attention. It was as though her earlier period of imposed darkness had made her appreciate every subtle beauty nature had to offer. Long country walks increased her stamina and her health continued to improve dramatically. As she walked, random thoughts about creation and other deep philosophical questions drifted, undisturbed, in and out of her mind. Gradually she found herself staring out towards the silver sea more frequently, and by the time she was sixteen Odette had made up her mind that she wanted to marry an Englishman and experience what life was like on the other side of the Channel. Furthermore, being a decidedly strong-willed young girl, she informed her mother accordingly!

Yvonne Brailly took her daughter's vow to marry an Englishman in her stride, since there was certain logic in her plan if she genuinely wanted to live in England. Besides, she knew her children well and had no doubt whatsoever that her daughter would follow a path of her own choosing. Even her school reports suggested as much. As far as she could tell, the nuns had observed her daughter and recorded her character traits with a great deal of accuracy. They had noted her intelligence, sense of humour and enthusiasm for life, along with her extreme obstinacy, occasional petulance and wilful determination. All these traits were marked in her final end of year report. The nuns had also observed with a hint of amusement that she was unlikely to embark on an ecclesiastical career! Yvonne meanwhile had recognised that in addition to her scholarly prowess Odette was accomplished in the art of cooking and in needlework. Nevertheless, she did not immerse herself in domestic duties very often, preferring instead to roam the countryside every evening until darkness descended.

In 1930 Odette passed through the imposing iron school gates for the last time. She was eighteen years old; yet her face still had the appearance of an eight-year-old. Although she had grown tall and had a slim, well-proportioned figure, her face displayed the chubby cheeks of childhood. These overly full cheeks, dark brown deep-set wide eyes, a lopsided grin and long wavy brown hair conspired to preserve her childhood appearance. This childlike façade was reinforced by a disarming naivety that belied her strong, intelligent nature.

Most evenings Odette would write in her journal. During this nightly ritual she usually recorded the details of her evening walks. She knew the coastline intimately and loved all of the seasonal changes, but spring was her favourite. The spring of 1930 was a special time for Odette. As she noted new flower shoots, buds on tree branches and other signs of new life awakening from the hibernation of a dreary, cold and predictably wet winter, she would ponder her future. She now considered herself to be a woman and her mind would sift through a list of attributes that her potential husband should possess. These included: being English, of course; a nice smile; a deep and sincere English voice; a kindly disposition; a good sense of humour; strong moral fibre; dependability; intelligence; and good dress sense.

With a disarming level of straightforward innocence and optimism Odette truly did believe that, by merely making a wish list, God or the universe would automatically deliver the goods. On this occasion her faith was well placed, for in the summer of that same year a romance blossomed between the young Odette and an Englishman called Roy Sansom. He was the son of a British officer who had been billeted with the Brailly family during the war and had returned to Normandy to improve his knowledge of the French language. Roy worked in the hotel industry and discreet checks on his background revealed no obvious character weaknesses. According to Grandmother Brailly, weak men were prone to gambling, alcoholism and womanising. Some women she had observed had been unfortunate enough to marry a man with all three of these vices! They were a constant source of worry, poverty and distress to a good many women. Fortunately, Roy Sansom was refined and restrained in his habits, although he was considerably older than his wife-to-be. This was Odette's first real romance and she was quite in awe of the Englishman. Their courtship was remarkably brief, and at the tender age of nineteen, in 1931, Odette married Roy at the Church of Saint Pierre. But despite her impatience for a new life in England she had to wait another year before she was taken across the Channel.

Notes

1   Imperial War Museum, oral history interview with Odette Hallowes, 1985.
2   *Ibid.*

2

ADOPTING ENGLAND

Odette's journey to England eventually began shortly after the birth of her first daughter Francoise in 1932, and the Sansom family made their home in Kensington, London. A second daughter named Lily arrived in 1934, and a third named Marianne was born in 1936. However, while Odette was largely preoccupied with the joys of motherhood, political tension was increasing yet again across Europe. The roots of this particular tension lay firmly in the aftermath of the First World War. German politics had polarised sharply in 1918 and there was a very real threat of a socialist revolution in Germany at this time. Widespread poverty and starvation, the influenza pandemic and a rise in the number of people suffering from tuberculosis and venereal disease, overwhelmed a nation that was still smarting from the humiliation of defeat and the harsh conditions of the Treaty of Versailles. Political and economic stability was achieved for a time in the shape of a newly formed democratic Weimar Republic under the guidance of Stresseman. The latter expressed peaceful intentions and even took Germany into the League of Nations in 1925. Indeed, despite the fact that Stresseman was secretly rearming Germany in preparation for another conflict, he nonetheless gave a fine speech to

the League propounding Germany's peaceful intentions.
All German stability collapsed when he died a few weeks
before the Wall Street Crash of 1929. During the uncertain
years of the Great Depression that followed, the German
people increasingly turned to the new ideology of fascism,
in the vain hope that fascists would restore Germany to her
former glory. Thus, with his sinister hatred of Jews, gypsies,
homosexuals and what he termed to be the feeble-minded,
the fascist leader of the Nazi party Adolf Hitler came to
power in 1933. Subsequently, Germany was plunged into a
moral abyss.

Odette read the newspapers avidly and listened anxiously
to radio broadcasts. The changing political face of Europe
was a source of constant concern. Civil war in Spain had
resulted in a fascist victory for General Franco, and the
Italians had embraced the fascist leader Mussolini. It seemed
to Odette that right-wing dictatorships were destined to
dominate the whole of Europe. Incredibly, some political
commentators even welcomed these changes, believing
that the march of fascism would stem the tide of socialism.
Events in Germany were particularly disturbing as the Nazis
burned books, persecuted Jews and threatened territorial
expansion to the east. In an attempt to avoid another war,
the British Prime Minister Neville Chamberlain and his
French counterpart Deladier decided to pursue a policy
of appeasement towards Hitler. Both took the view that it
was important to avoid conflict on humanitarian grounds.
Besides which, neither Britain nor France was prepared for
war. The economy of both countries had not recovered from
the previous conflict and it would have been foolish not to
have attempted a political compromise. At the very least,
the policy of appeasement would buy Britain and France

some valuable time in which to rearm for war. Furthermore, although both countries were deeply disturbed by the rampant anti-Semitism that had infiltrated German society at all levels, Hitler's territorial demands did not seem particularly unreasonable at this time.

Under the terms of the Versailles Treaty Germany had been forced to relinquish an area of land called the Sudetenland to the state of Czechoslovakia. Hitler was demanding that this area should be returned to Germany. Chamberlain and Deladier both agreed that this was not an unreasonable request and the land was duly returned to German rule at the Munich Conference in 1938. Hitler firmly assured Chamberlain and Deladier that his territorial claims were restricted to the Sudetenland. British and French citizens alike heaved a collective sigh of relief and celebrated the successful negotiations with street parties. Then, without warning, the Nazis marched into Czechoslovakia in March 1939. Appeasement was dead. Like many others, Odette feared for her children and the future of Europe. But neither Britain nor France intended to stand by and let Hitler rampage across Europe and the former signed an Anglo-Polish agreement in August 1939. With this pact, the stage was set for war, since the agreement promised British military aid to Poland in the event of an invasion. Therefore, when Germany invaded Poland on 1 September 1939 as part of a planned strategy to gain German living space in the east, Britain and France responded by declaring war on Germany on 3 September.

Despite this declaration of war Britain was plunged into a strange limbo for a few months. This period became known as the 'Phoney War'. Hitler's attention was concentrated on Eastern Europe and nothing seemed to be happening in the west. Children, pregnant women and hospital patients were evacuated from the cities and resettled into the countryside; people practised gas mask drills and adhered to the black-out rules, cinemas were closed and young men and women were enlisted into the armed forces, but nothing of any note actually happened. In fact, more accidents happened because of the black-outs than because of war activity. Even ninety per cent of the evacuees were back home by Christmas. There were publicly voiced rumours that Chamberlain was still trying to negotiate a separate peace deal with Hitler, but Odette was unsure of the foundations for this gossip so gave the rumours little credence. Against all advice to the contrary she had chosen to remain in Kensington with her children when war was declared. Her husband Roy had been one of the first to enlist in the armed forces and Odette had simply adapted to his absence and focused on the needs of her children. Life appeared to continue much as it had done before Chamberlain's declaration of war.

This 'calm before the storm' came to an abrupt end in April 1940 when the British were defeated in their Norwegian Campaign. There followed a rapid chain of events that shook the populations of Britain and France. On 10 May the Germans invaded the Netherlands, Belgium and Luxembourg. Neville Chamberlain resigned as British Prime Minister and was replaced by Winston Churchill. On 12 May the Germans put paid to the idea that they were only interested in expanding their territories eastwards and crossed the border into France. Between 26 May and 4 June British and French troops were hurriedly evacuated from Dunkirk. This process required nearly 900 ships, some of which were privately owned. Between them they ferried almost 340,000 troops back to Britain. By 14 June the

Germans had taken over and gained control of Paris. Odette began to feel uneasy in her London home and continued to listen earnestly to the radio for news of France. Yet as she watched her children playing in Kensington Gardens, bathed in sunlight and swathed in the green leaves of summer, she still found it almost impossible to believe that the world was at war. Unsure of what she could do for the war effort at this stage, she gave away a family heirloom, her pride and joy:

> I sent my French coffee pot to be melted and that was that, I tried to forget about it all for a moment.[1]

Britain had been lulled into a false sense of security by the Phoney War, but its population responded with great courage when the defence of the realm began in earnest. Morale was high and most British people complained more about the weather than they did about German bombs. The French leader Marshal Pétain was eighty-two years old and had little mental or physical strength with which to fight the Nazis. He surrendered France to Germany and formed an official government in Vichy in central France. Northern France was occupied by German forces while southern France was policed by the Gestapo and Vichy police. The Vichy government collaborated fully with the Nazis and also attempted to recruit young Frenchmen into the German armed forces.

It was at this point that Hitler turned his attention towards Britain. However, Germany could not invade Britain until the Luftwaffe had achieved air supremacy. Consequently, the Battle of Britain, which began on 10 July 1940, was crucial. It was the first battle to be decided by air power alone and the subsequent German defeat forced Hitler to abandon Operation Sea Lion, which was the code name for the planned invasion of Britain. By the end of September the German Luftwaffe had lost 1,408 aircraft compared with Britain's loss of 697 aircraft. The Luftwaffe dropped a few bombs on British cities in August 1940, but between 7 September 1940 and May 1941 all major cities were subjected to unremitting waves of aerial bombardment. Over 80,000 civilian casualties were sustained during this period. During the frequent air raids of September 1940 Odette sat with her children in the makeshift Anderson shelter at the bottom of their garden. They held hands and sang songs while they waited for the 'all clear' siren. But the uncertainty and danger began to take its toll. The faces of her daughters grew strained, their lips pinched and their eyes anxious. While she firmly believed that she should not be forced out of her comfortable home by the Nazis, common sense rather than stubborn resistance finally won the day. After a tense and fretful month, she moved her family to rented accommodation in Somerset.

The tiny picture postcard village of Red Ball was on the border of Somerset and Devon, and Odette managed to find rooms in an old cottage that overlooked the valley. A short distance away her mother-in-law had rented a room in a small guest house, and since the two were firm friends they spent a lot of time together over the following weeks. They swapped gossip, local news, snippets of information about the war, some true, some embellished, and waited apprehensively for news of Yvonne, Louis and Roy. Weeks and months drifted by in a never-ending round of washing, cleaning, cooking and shopping, getting the girls ready for school, mending clothes that were torn by the hedgerows, sticking elastoplasts on cut knees, knitting scarves for the troops, digging the garden to plant vegetables, feeding the chickens and collecting their eggs; there always seemed to be something to do. Like most women living on the home front Odette was involved in digging for victory, salvaging paper and other household waste items for the war effort and working a few hours a week for the women's voluntary services. Life was sometimes difficult because rationing limited the types of meals that could be prepared for the family. Women were encouraged to be frugal and creative with their wartime recipes, and a radio doctor was employed by the government's Ministry of Food to extol the virtues of simple home-grown food. By 1941 women were being conscripted into the armed forces and most of those left in the village either worked as land girls in the surrounding countryside or had headed for the cities to swell the ranks of those working in the munitions factories.

Odette found that taking care of her children and her mother-in-law was a full-time occupation, and after a hectic day she often knitted and sewed long into the night to make clothes for her daughters. Some respite from this non-stop whirlwind of activity was gained during long, peaceful country walks. An area called the 'Tippings' near the village of Culmstock was a favourite family haunt. Here, on the mound of a quiet hillside it was possible to see for miles: the gentle, rolling hills that covered the landscape like a patchwork quilt, the apple orchards and oak trees in the distance, lazy cattle grazing aimlessly in the distance and the little muddy tracks that led up to Culmstock Beacon. Here it was possible for Odette to note the changing colours of the wild flowers and hedgerows and view the most beautiful sunrise on a clear morning. In autumn the spectacular views were accompanied by the smell of smouldering bonfires, wet blackberry bushes and slushy multicoloured leaves.

The girls grew stronger and less tense. They had settled quickly and easily into the village school which had been flooded with evacuees. The school operated a shift system whereby local children attended classes in the morning and evacuee children in the afternoon. Space was limited and Odette's daughters, along with other village school children, were taken on lengthy nature rambles to alleviate severe overcrowding in the classrooms. Sometimes it was possible for the children to watch distant aerial battles from safe hill-top positions. Inevitably the war invaded the school curriculum, with 'Wings for Victory' and 'Salute the Soldier' weeks taking their place alongside other fundraising activities. Children who raised the most money, or brought the most books to school for the soldiers, were given a stripe to stick on their arm. Teachers did make concerted efforts, along with parents, to protect children from the horrors of war, but since most children had a father, brother or uncle taking part in the conflict it was difficult to afford them much protection in this respect. Some children had also experienced the loss of a relative, and in these particularly distressing circumstances teachers felt inclined to give some basic explanation of why Britain was at war. Most teachers and parents believed that children were less likely to worry if they were kept occupied and given the opportunity to help the fighting forces by fund-raising and making clothes. Balaclavas, gloves, socks, pullovers and scarves were among the vast array of clothing knitted by children, many of whom were taught to read and knit at the same time.

Odette took part in many of the fund-raising events and began to make friends with the inhabitants of Culmstock. In London there had been considerable anti-French feeling after the fall of France. Londoners had expressed a very real and heartfelt resentment that Britain's only ally had failed them. France had possessed the only army on the continent of Europe capable of withstanding a German attack. The speed at which German forces had invaded and taken possession of her beloved homeland had shocked the British people, and they were not averse to voicing their disappointment. Derogatory comments about the French people were frequently directed at her in the London marketplaces and succeeded in wounding her pride. Shopping had become a bit of an ordeal, but in Culmstock they didn't simply tolerate her; the villagers eventually welcomed Odette and her family into their community. Here in this tiny village there were old men who had fought alongside the French during the First World War, and they seemed to understand that no country had been fully prepared for the German onslaught. Despite this welcome, however, Odette felt restless. It was a feeling that originated from impotence. To date, all she had done was donate a pint of blood and a fine, vintage, French aluminium coffee pot. True, the latter was an extremely painful sacrifice, since it had been in her family for generations, but it was not very much compared to the people who were clearly risking their lives.

Country life seemed far removed from the war. Food and clothing was rationed and the village seemed to be preoccupied with a new influx of evacuees from Bristol, but generally morale was high. It was now the end of November 1941 and Odette had spent a lot of time in recent months nursing her mother-in-law. It transpired that old Mrs Sansom had been suffering from tuberculosis in secret for some time. With the onset of the winter months she no longer had the strength to fight the illness. Day after day

Odette washed her, brushed and set her hair, read to her and coaxed her to eat. She gleefully reminded her that Hitler had invaded Russia back in June and newspaper reports were convinced that the German army would now perish in the bitter Russian winter. On 7 December she'd rushed to tell her that the Japanese had attacked Pearl Harbor, and assured her that now the Americans had entered the war a German defeat was only a matter of time. But all the encouragement in the world could not breathe new life and vigour into the fragile old lady, and in late December she died quietly in her bed.

As Britain entered the fourth year of the war, Odette sat motionless in the living room of the Somerset cottage, surrounded by tiny oil lamps, china ornaments, a ticking grandfather clock and a collection of horse and hound-type pictures that were hung precariously on the four walls. The girls were asleep and she had finished the darning of socks for the evening. She studiously watched the grandfather clock and reflected on the changing course of the war and the fate of her beloved France. Surely now, in 1942, things were bound to improve. How could Hitler possibly hope to take on the might of the Russians *and* the Americans? Britain had been remarkable in holding out against the odds for so long, but what would happen now? As for France, could she ever live down the shame of Marshal Pétain's Vichy government? Could anyone restore the honour of France when French collaborators had attacked British ships on the orders of the Wehrmacht? General de Gaulle had rallied the Free French in an amazing and inspiring speech, and was doing his best to claw back some respect for France, but how on earth was this possible?

Odette's basic analysis of the war was based, like any other housewife, on newspaper reports and radio broadcasts. Much of this she knew to be propaganda. All news reports were heavily censored and most were constructed in such a way as to boost morale. Sometimes she would sit at her kitchen table and try to discern precisely the course that the war was taking; while at other times she would dismiss her general thoughts of war and focus on her memories of her mother and brother. There had been no news of them since the Germans took over Paris. Were they injured? Were they homeless or even dead? Were they trying to contact her, desperate for her help? Such thoughts, she knew, were futile, they simply fired through her mind like electric currents on a worn-out circuit. During such periods of doubt and concern she would remember, with some affection and amusement, her grandfather's stern caution about self-pity and destructive thoughts. Conjuring up a mental image of her stoical Grandfather Brailly, she would reprimand herself sternly for giving in to such negative feelings.

Notes

1 Imperial War Museum, oral history interview with Odette Hallowes, 1985.

3

BAKER STREET SPECIALS

It was a day much like any other when Odette, who was busy sorting out her laundry, overheard a radio appeal that was to change the course of her life forever. The same appeal also found its way into the evening newspapers. In preparation for an Allied invasion of Europe, members of the War Office were keen to discover the intricacies of the French coastline. With this objective in mind they had launched a public appeal for photographs of France. A dutiful Odette quickly responded to this request, bundled up a batch of family photographs and promptly dispatched them. This innocent action constituted her first step on the road towards the British Special Operations Executive (SOE).

This establishment was responsible for all forms of espionage during the Second World War. The headquarters of SOE was based at 64 Baker Street, London, and was formed on 19 July 1940 from a small number of pre-existing intelligence services. Winston Churchill was apt to refer to SOE agents as the 'Baker Street Specials'. In addition to the offices in Baker Street, the SOE also inhabited a discreet area of Portman Square. Its employees generally referred to the organisation as 'The Firm' and it was divided into different sections, each responsible for a separate area of Europe. Their remit was, in

Churchill's words, 'To Set Europe Ablaze.' Agents were required to disrupt Nazi war aims by any means possible and galvanise the native populations of occupied territories into taking action against their conquerers.

But the SOE was not without its detractors. Naturally the British wanted to secure an ultimate Allied victory over the Nazis, but there was considerable political opposition to the methods proposed by the SOE. Some ministers thought it was simply 'not quite British' to get involved in things such as sabotage and undercover work on such a grand scale. They said there was something quite distasteful about the whole process.

However, it was clear to the military Chiefs of Staff, who were contemplating an invasion of Europe, that the populations of occupied Europe needed to be prepared for such an invasion. They needed to get patriots on side to assist in the fight against Germany. As one of the SOE lectures on the value of operational propaganda asserted:

Today it is useless for our propaganda merely to persuade Frenchmen that the Boche is a swine. It must also instruct Frenchmen how to kick the Boche out of France. Our propaganda to enemy and occupied countries is now mainly operational; and, as such, should always contain the joint elements of persuasion and action.[1]

The French, in particular, were very important in terms of military strategy. Any British invasion of the continent would naturally involve France. But how would the French feel about such an invasion? To what extent did the Vichy government command the loyalty of ordinary French people? How many in occupied France could be persuaded to fight with Britain when the time was right? How much support could General de Gaulle and the Free French rely on? What was morale like in France? Was it possible to effectively train the French to use British weapons in time for an invasion? How easy would it be to disrupt Nazi communication lines, transport and supply networks? What were their exact geographical positions? Where were their armament stores? All these questions, and more, needed to be answered before the next Allied phase of military strategy could be implemented. In addition to 'Setting Europe Ablaze', therefore, SOE French Section, like its Section counterparts, was primarily responsible for acquiring vital information.

When talking about her accidental recruitment into the SOE, Odette explained:

It was by mistake really. I sent the photographs to the wrong address. I think I sent them to the navy when they should have gone to the army. In any case they reached where they were supposed to be going. I thought them to be useless really, most of no use to anybody, just photographs of myself and my brother on the beaches of Boulogne and Calais. I was very surprised when I received a letter thanking me for the photographs and asking if it was possible for me to attend an interview in London. I went of course, because I thought that at least that way I would get my photographs back! When I arrived for the interview I was asked a lot of questions and the men said that they had been making enquiries about me in Britain and France and they were very satisfied with my background.

I lost my temper and said 'Why did you have to make enquiries about me? What do you think I am?' They told me to calm down and said 'You do not know this but we train people here, we train them and send them back to their countries to help us get information. Women are very useful in this respect.' Well I could see that – I agreed with all that, so I said 'I think women are very useful anyway.' That did it! Then they said 'Well we are glad that you think that way because we are going to ask you to become one of them.' Then they told me a bit about the work they were doing. Of course I wanted to help the war effort and I offered to do some translation or something else along those lines, but when they told me what they wanted me to do I told them that it was just not possible. I told them 'I have children, my children come first. Besides, you must be of a certain type to do this thing. I haven't got the brain for it and there are physical things that are necessary for the job, it is absolutely not possible. They told me to go away and think about it, and I did. They did not pressure me, they were clever that way, and they knew that I would be in two minds. I was really, very tormented.[2]

Captain Selwyn Jepson and Major Maurice Buckmaster were the two men who interviewed the very youthful-looking Odette. Indeed, the latter expressed extreme surprise at the mention of her three children as Odette recalled:

One of the first things he said to me when I spoke about my children was: 'Good God! You still look like a child yourself.' In those days I used to look much younger than my years. I looked very childish, and I was, I suppose – I was a bit childish too.[3]

Buckmaster had previously served as an intelligence officer with the 50th Division and was now in charge of the French Section of the SOE. He was assisted by an extremely efficient, level-headed and brilliant woman named Vera Atkins. All SOE agents were recruited in much the same manner. Backgrounds of suitable people were carefully checked and selection invitation letters posted. Potential recruits were subsequently interviewed at the Hotel Victoria in room 238 and decisions made on both sides. Women were particularly valuable as spies behind enemy lines because they could move about more freely without question. For example, if a man was roaming about the streets in German-occupied territory he was more likely to be questioned by the Gestapo. He would need a very good cover to explain his presence, especially in broad daylight, because most men were fully occupied in the workplace or the military.

In contrast, it was perfectly acceptable for women to be busying themselves about the streets; they had families to shop for, children and relatives to attend to. Even in country areas, women could explain away a bicycle ride across fields and forests by arguing that they were collecting eggs or milk from a farm, or picking fruit for a family pie. Cultural expectations also favoured the position of female spies. German women were expected to remain in the domestic sphere and bring forth children for Hitler's Fatherland. For many members of the Gestapo, therefore, it was inconceivable that a woman would want to engage in espionage work. By the end of the war this blinkered view had no doubt shifted.

Being an intelligent French national Odette fitted the requirements of the SOE perfectly. But the work of secret agents was fraught with danger. During her initial interviews Odette recalled that both Jepson and Buckmaster were kindly men who took great care to outline the nature of their work without giving away any detail. They emphasised the dangers and the fact that some of their agents had not returned from their assignments. During her train journey back to Somerset she had no illusions. Espionage was a treacherous and difficult business, a world where nobody could be fully trusted. To some extent her views on this remained fixed:

> It is a game that I suppose is a good game for certain people. A game of youth, you have to have ideals. You have to have the mental strength and the physical fitness for it. But it is not possible for it ever to be a clean game.[4]

The tentacles of the SOE were far-reaching and some agents were trained in the Mediterranean. In Britain the SOE provided around 13,500 courses for about 6,800 students, the overwhelming majority of whom were nationals of enemy-occupied countries. Only 480 of them were British.[5] Once recruited, agents were trained in paramilitary schools across Britain. Some of the first of these schools were housed in the mansions and shooting lodges of Scotland. Parachute training took place at airfields across the length and breadth of the country and was largely dependent on the unpredictable British weather. On completion of training, agents were given their various assignments and Vera Atkins did much of the administrative work from that point on. She supplied agents with practical field information, and ensured that small but important details were taken care of, such as French clothing labels for British garments, false identity papers, passports, and photographs of bogus family members. Vera was an administrator *par excellence*; no detail escaped her attention and she was renowned for having a photographic memory. Agents were transported into France in a number of ways. Some were parachuted into the occupied territory, while others travelled to Gibraltar first and then made their way into France by way of naval vessels. Indeed, it was much easier to get agents into France than it was to get them back again.

Around the time that Odette attended her first interview in 1942 there were over twenty officers working undercover in France. The centre of the French Resistance movement was Lille, but British agents and Resistance fighters were operational in a variety of occupied and unoccupied areas. French patriots were understandably impatient and anxious to reclaim their country. Consequently they were apt to be impulsive and reckless at times. British agents needed to curb the eagerness of the French and train and co-ordinate the Resistance movements in readiness for an Allied invasion. In addition they concentrated on disrupting Nazi war efforts whenever possible and gathering crucial information. British weapons, radio equipment and supplies were airlifted into France by Lysander aircraft to be distributed to the various undercover circuits. For security reasons no agent was able to use the ordinary telephone for communication purposes; all units and individual agents were totally reliant on their radio operators. Without them, there could be no connection with London, and any operational strategy would effectively collapse. Yet radio operators were sometimes forced to 'go to ground' for security reasons and it often took a considerable time for them to resurface. Conditions in the field could be very difficult. Courier agents were forced to use bicycles to ferry information from one place to another. It was extremely hazardous to own a car because of the extra paperwork involved. Cars required black market petrol and since this was a commodity dangerous to obtain it drew unnecessary attention to undercover activities. Communication problems worsened as circuit networks expanded. It became virtually impossible for couriers to cycle a hundred or so kilometres in time to inform various groups about expected Royal Air Force parachute drops. These RAF deliveries were dictated by other operational concerns that could alter on a daily, and sometimes hourly, basis. Flights were also dependent on changing weather conditions, but it was important for agents to let their groups know whether a delivery was 'on' or 'off'.

By 1942 the French Section of the SOE was expanding its influence daily and good agents were urgently needed. Everyone was a volunteer and no pressure was brought to bear on potential recruits. But as Odette had already acknowledged to herself, it did take a certain kind of person to be an accomplished spy. There were very few people who were suitable for undercover work, and even fewer who possessed that special integrity that was so vital for achieving operational success and developing a sense of comradeship. Consequently, she took a long time to make up her mind about joining the SOE and had certain misgivings. To begin with she was not at all convinced that she was capable of being a spy. All through her childhood years she had suffered from illnesses so naturally she questioned her physical stamina. There was also the question of a woman's place in society. Women were playing a vital role in munitions factories and on the land, but spying? This was a different matter entirely. But her fears and concerns were primarily for her children, not for herself. For months she had wanted to do more for the war effort, to play her part in the overthrow of the Nazis. She had now been offered an opportunity to do just that, but the decision was not easy. Odette talked over her dilemma with her husband:

> Of course he was insulted! But he left the decision to me and the War Office people, he did not try and influence me. He agreed that I could do the training, and if I was found to be acceptable he said that I could do this thing. You see, I had two reasons for wanting to help. After all I was French born, and the Germans had overrun my country. I also wanted to help England because I was married to an Englishman and my children were English.[6]

Understandably, Roy Sansom was extremely upset that his wife, and the mother of his three children, was contemplating the prospect of entering the world of espionage. In the 1930s and '40s women barely stepped out of the domestic environment. Even when they entered the work place they were forced to resign on marriage. Although the marriage bar had now been lifted in some quarters to pave the way for female war work, it still went completely against the grain for a man to think of his wife as a spy. The consensus of contemporary male opinion would have argued that it was simply not a woman's place to go fooling around Europe getting involved in spying and sabotage. The mere suggestion that his wife was urgently required for crucial undercover work severely undermined all traditional notions of masculinity. In effect, Roy Sansom was being forced to accept the uncomfortable idea that his own war service was probably of less importance than the contribution that could be made by his wife.

Odette was fully aware of her husband's wounded pride, but for her there were wider and more important issues at stake. Describing her mental turmoil, it became clear that her final decision was influenced by other events that were taking place across the Channel:

> I thought about it for months and months. Then I received some very bad news. A Red Cross messenger informed me that my brother was wounded and lay in a military hospital in Paris. The Nazis had also taken my family home. My mother had been forced to leave her home and for the second time in her life she had lost everything to the Germans.[7]

On hearing this news Odette spent the following few weeks watching her children play and thinking about the children of Europe. English or French, it did not matter in the great scheme of things. Both nations were side-by-side in the war, and the liberation of Europe depended as much on an Anglo-French alliance as it did on American and Russian troops.

> I felt terrible. Then I thought, I am in the safety of beautiful Somerset, but am I going to be satisfied to accept, just like that, the fact that other people are going to suffer and get killed to, let's face it, get freedom for my children? Would I be satisfied not to lift a finger? I thought that if I were in France I could already be captured along with my children, but because I was in England I had an excuse to do nothing. It would be easy for me to do nothing, to think that way. I was happy under those beautiful trees in Somerset and wanted to stay there with my children. But then I thought, what if everyone thought like that? Will I be satisfied living out my life like this, knowing that other people were losing their lives while I did nothing? What if nobody risked anything? Am I going to be satisfied just staying put with my children? I knew that I had to do something, or at least I should try to do something. I thought that if I tried to do the training and they discovered that I could not do it, perhaps they would send me to do some translation work or maybe they would send me back home to my knitting![8]

With a steely determination and a sense of resignation she had uttered a prayer heavenwards.

> I thought … there is nobody left in my family to fight for the freedom of France now. My brother was in hospital, and nobody knew where my mother was, there was just me! I thought it is my duty to do what I can. I must at least try to do something. If I did the training and they said that I was not

suitable, then at least I would know that I tried. There was always that feeling that I was brought up with, a feeling that one must do one's duty, not only to honour my father but also a duty to my country.[9]

Odette's innate sense of duty eventually prevailed over her immediate family concerns. For her, both the family's honour and the honour of France were at stake and she could not possibly refuse to help. Having made up her mind, Odette made arrangements for her children to be cared for at the convent of St Helen in Essex. She then telephoned Captain Jepson to inform him of her decision and express her deep-seated reservations. Stating her position in no uncertain terms, she told him rather abruptly: 'I am prepared do the training and then you will see that I am not the right person.'[10]

Notes

1 Rigden, D., *SOE Syllabus: Lessons in Ungentlemanly Warfare* (Richmond, 2004), p. 192.

2 Imperial War Museum, oral history interview with Odette Hallowes, 1985.

3 *Ibid.*

4 *Ibid.*

5 Rigden, *SOE Syllabus: Lessons in Ungentlemanly Warfare*, p. 17.

6 Imperial War Museum, oral history interview with Odette Hallowes, 1985.

7 *Ibid.*

8 *Ibid.*

9 *Ibid.*

10 *Ibid.*

BECOMING A SPY

As a prerequisite to working for the SOE, Odette was required to join the First Aid Nursing Yeomanry and swap her elegant suits and motherly pinafores for a uniform of khaki. She was not overly keen on wearing a uniform, even though khaki, she'd noted with some satisfaction, appeared to suit her. On her arrival at the training school she still felt somewhat bemused by the situation that she found herself in. Here she was; a French housewife and mother, and one who was rather naive in many respects. She had married young and knew nothing very much about the world or politics, only that the Nazi creed was evil and that her country had been overrun by them. True, she was intelligent and determined, but would this be enough? Gently she had touched her bare throat with her slim manicured fingers. The Gestapo were fond of hanging captured agents after they had finished torturing them. She did not suppose she would get given the choice of how she died, but decided there and then that she would much prefer a firing squad than a rope. Surely that method was quicker.

Odette consoled herself with the knowledge that at least the Gestapo would not know of her children. Neither could the Gestapo, with all their methods of terror and torture, succeed in breaking her heart. This had already been broken a week earlier when she had left her children at St Helen's convent school. Recalling the moment when she had reluctantly parted with her daughters, Odette spoke in a subdued voice:

> Yes that was the thing – it was the only thing – my heart was broken at leaving them. I thought that with all of the things the Gestapo can do now it will only be physical, they cannot break what is already broken.[1]

To ease what she knew would be a long absence, Odette also deposited a large number of letters with the nuns, to give to the children on a regular basis, and explained to them that she was needed to help the war effort. They'd pleaded with her to return soon and she'd hugged them closely, giving them unnecessary instructions on how to behave, how to keep warm, how to eat well and how to take care of each other while she was away. Then she had given them a big broad smile and a wave before turning towards the convent gates. There was a lump in her throat so big that she could hardly breathe, but she'd choked back her tears until, in the privacy of the little cottage, the floodgates opened. The next morning, puffy-eyed from crying the night before, she'd looked in the mirror at her bloated, tear-stained face and tried with all her might to quash her emotions. There were certain things she had to do and certain ways she needed to think if she was going to be of any use to France at all.

There were several SOE training schools dotted around the country, although most were situated in the western Highlands of Scotland. Agents were required to undergo four stages of training, which included attendance at a preliminary school, a paramilitary school, finishing school and a briefing station. Preliminary schools taught basic weapons handling, unarmed combat and elementary map-reading skills, and essentially they filtered out those individuals who were not suitable for progression to commando-style training. The paramilitary schools focused on military defence techniques, and how to perform raids on enemy bases such as Gestapo headquarters, alongside procedures for silent killing and methods of sabotage. It was in these schools that agents acquired foreign weapons training and in-depth knowledge of enemy organisations. Morse code and procedures for attacking ports and ships also featured strongly on the varied curriculum. At the finishing schools agents were instructed on how to assume and maintain their new undercover identities. They also learnt how to recruit Resistance workers, organise a group of agents and communicate in a clandestine and unobtrusive fashion. Briefing stations represented the last hurdle before going into the field, and it was here that agents received their final instructions and were given precise details of their individual missions. There were other more specialised SOE training schools that were designed to develop expertise in certain areas, such as micro photography, subversive propaganda, advanced sabotage techniques, and security tuition for those concerned with new wireless radio equipment and radar. But the bulk of agents followed the basic four-stage programme before beginning their work.

Much of Odette's training took place in a large country mansion situated in a very secluded part of the New Forest. Nestled among the myriad of trees there was a beautiful lake surrounded by Victorian-style sculptures of bygone heroes and ornamental flower containers. All recruits were asked to choose a new name for their training period and were given a code number. Their training was rigorous and, at times, difficult. Odette chose her middle name Celine for the purpose of the training school programme. The eight o'clock start was something she was used to, since she'd always risen early to get her girls to school on time. The day began with physical training and was followed by a variety of lectures. Recruits were taught how to decipher codes, how to map-read accurately and how to measure air fields for RAF landings. The Hudson aircraft, for instance, required more landing space than the Lysander. They had practical lessons in unarmed combat and endured daily target practice with Sten guns. Canoe lessons were given during the hours of darkness, and by the end of the course all recruits could steer a canoe without making a single sound. They were also taught poaching and survival skills, such as finding one's direction by the position of the stars.

Odette became adept at the art of disguise, laughing uncontrollably at the sight of her image in some of the wigs. She could age herself by forty years if necessary, with the aid of special make-up and careful application techniques. Disguise was not merely about make-up and other such visible aids, it was about being able to adopt a character in total. This process involved training the mind to think in different ways, learning to walk with a different gait, discovering how to speak with an alien accent, and practising certain habits and mannerisms that would be in tune with the new character. Odette found the process fascinating, even the gadgetry provided an endless source of interest. The use of exploding pens, matchboxes and sabotage equipment became second nature to her. More importantly, she began to notice a change in herself. For the first time ever she felt a sense of a wider belonging – what some people chose to call the *esprit de corps*. Now she had comrades. They possessed a shared sense of purpose and history. There was an almost tangible connection between her and others who had gone before her in the First Aid Nursing Yeomanry. This was an unexpected but most welcome feeling.

Through the arduous weeks of training the recruits ached, cringed, laughed, and cried together. They were a lively group of vibrant, pretty young women, who supported each other without reservation. The New Forest, with its dark, thickly wooded landscape and tranquil lakes, had become their home from home. They consoled each other when things got tough, or an instructor seemed heavy-handed; and applauded each other when things went well, such as when three bullseyes were scored at target practice. Nicknames were given to instructors and faces pulled in grimaces behind their backs. At the end of each day they exchanged confidences, and shared their hopes and dreams for the future. There was a mutual respect and understanding between these new SOE members, and Odette felt proud to be counted among their number.

Naturally, academic and practical lectures were designed to prepare agents physically and mentally for the tasks that lay ahead. The following extracts are taken from a basic lecture framework, which provided agents with essential guidelines on how to develop an informant service within enemy-occupied territory:

Without good information it is impossible to protect oneself from the enemy or to plan or time operations. You need to know local conditions e.g. the danger of ordering wrong drinks or cigarettes. Transport services and restrictions. You need to provide a good reason for travelling. Avoid market days when there is a danger of a search for 'black market' goods. Understand new slang or colloquialisms brought about by war, and the general temper of the local population.

Check that your identity papers are in order. Find out how to procure ration cards. Discover what passes are necessary to overcome movement restrictions. Are the control posts manned by enemy troops or local police? Clarify evacuation procedures from forbidden zones and observe curfew hours and blackout regulations. Check licenses and travel restrictions.

Observe the enemy methods and their personnel. Locate their troop positions and that of the Gestapo. Find out the attitude of the local police. Are there any civilian police spies or agents provocateurs? If so, find out their names.

Decide on possible targets: enemy communications, Headquarters, supply dumps and factories. Are there any bottlenecks in enemy production? What are the internal workings of the factories, power stations, railways and communication networks? Get to know the personnel employed in these areas, the means of entry, layout of machines, number of guards and control systems. Find out what documents or workers passes are needed to gain access to these targets.

This information is obtained by direct interrogation, constant personal observation, reading newspapers and listening to radio and by cultivating an informant service.

The Informant Service:
Very few should know that they are informants. The great bulk will be quite unconscious of it. Select people from as many strata of society, trades and professions as possible.

Best people are those who constantly mix with all sorts. These include: priests, innkeepers, waitresses and barmaids, doctors, dentists and hospital staffs, postmen, telephone and telegraph operators, bankers, shopkeepers, railway officials and workers, servants and all grumblers and malcontents. In due course you may decide to approach a few of the more trustworthy informants with a view to recruiting them.

You need to be able to develop a technique of eaves-dropping on the masses. An ability to hear and separate two simultaneous conversations while ostensibly listening to a third. Take advantage of other people's bad security, for example – careless talk, disgruntled enemy personnel, affecting ignorance and thus encouraging others to air their knowledge and making false statements to elicit correct reply. Do not discourage informants however trivial the information.[2]

The SOE syllabus was extensive and covered numerous topics. These included: objects and methods of irregular warfare, general security and advanced security for wireless operators, informant services, cover, make-up and disguise, observation, objects and methods of counter-espionage, descriptions and surveillance, personal and house searches, burglary, interrogation, agent management, organisation, cell systems and operations, communications, passive resistance, subversion of troops, allied propaganda, the principles of mechanics, tactics and field craft, codes and ciphers, demolitions and sabotage techniques, physical training and close combat and the use of secret inks. There were also in-depth lectures that described and explained the set-up and administration of the Nazi Party, German army and German police and intelligence services.[3]

Odette threw her heart and soul into the training course, but was impatient to get on with the job for real. All the recruits were enthusiastic, but Odette was more impatient than most to get over to France. The only aspect of the programme that she detested was the physical training:

> I was never any good at it really but the training overall was very good. The preparation of one's mind was very good. I was intrigued and fascinated by it, the pattern of it all. They even woke us up in the middle of the night to test our reactions. There were eight or ten men dressed in Nazi uniform and they staged a mock interrogation. The preparation was quite good.[4]

Odette remained convinced that her lack of physical prowess was a real hindrance to her overall training. This belief was confirmed during her parachute training at Ringway near Manchester. The graduates of the New Forest had been undergoing parachute training for several days and their typical day began at seven o'clock in the morning and continued until six in the evening. Every day began with an exercise regime and 'tumbling practice' as they all took turns to simulate parachute landings. One by one they followed each other onto the coconut mats, climbed the ladder and launched themselves through holes, with their knees clenched together, elbows glued to their sides, and heads tucked well in to their chests. They were submitted to several medical examinations in order to assess their fitness levels and they visited a number of 'dropping zones' to observe other parachutists in action. The prospect of leaping out of an aircraft was not one that appealed to any of them. Yet they cheerfully put themselves through the paces and coped with the practice descents the best they could.

Their capable instructor repeatedly informed them, with a vast array of accompanying hand gestures, that providing there was no crosswind, and they had mastered the art of handling their lift webs, they should experience no problem. Ideally, they would glide down to earth like a beautiful silk scarf. He then took great pains to explain that they also needed to hide their silk scarf very quickly in the bushes as soon as they landed. He tapped the blackboard with a long cane and discussed at length various wind currents and the types of dropping zones. Odette was prone to yawning discreetly during such lectures, often because she was exhausted. Nevertheless, she was determined to continue with the overall programme despite her particular aversion to physical training.

All recruits were required to make four parachute descents, two from a hot air balloon and two from a Whitley aircraft. Practice jumps were made from a constructed model that was based on a Whitley. When Odette heard the instructor yell out her name, she ascended the ladder as quickly as she could. Tiredness threatened to overcome her, but she rushed along the fuselage, assumed position and jumped. With an almighty crunch she fell to the ground and grabbed the side of her face. In her haste, she had smashed her face on the side of the hole as she'd jumped. Worse still, as she tried to stand up, a sharp pain shot up her right leg as though she had just received a knife wound. The hangar fell silent as the instructor lifted and supported her into the standing position. Dismissing the class with a mutter and a wave of his hand, he escorted the hobbling Odette to the medical room. An RAF medical officer quickly confirmed that she was suffering from concussion and a wrenched ankle. He was a young, handsome man, who was used to dealing with injuries such as Odette's on a daily basis. He ordered X-rays to confirm his diagnosis and Odette, who was still grimacing from the pain, had managed to give him a wane smile. At that particular point she had felt a bit giddy and was seriously worried that she might vomit all over the medic at any moment. Lying on her bed some time later, with her foot elevated on a soft white pillow, she'd stared at the ceiling and wondered if she would ever get over to France.

The following morning Odette awoke with a thumping headache and could only see out of one eye; the other had been forced closed by facial swelling. Peering reluctantly down at her ankle she could see that the swelling had subsided a little, though the bruising that had appeared overnight had turned it a deep shade of purple. A cursory visit from the medical officer later that morning confirmed, however, that it was simply a sprain. The MO further assured her that although he wanted her to see an ophthalmic specialist because of her swollen face, injuries such as hers were commonplace in training. He had stared out of Odette's window absent-mindedly while he was talking to her, seemingly preoccupied with aircraft that were taking off in the distance. Then he'd given her a broad smile, ruffled her hair as though she were a small child and briskly left the room. Odette briefly wondered if he had left prematurely because all the planes were now airborne and the view from her window was considerably less interesting than when he'd first entered her room. She had wanted to tell him about her headache, ask him for some painkillers, and question him about whether she still needed to keep her ankle elevated on the pillow. But his preoccupation with the view had distracted her and she cursed herself silently for her lack of assertiveness. With an air of resignation, Odette plumped up her pillow and turned onto her side; and as far as the pain in her ankle would allow, she tried to sleep.

A few days later Odette was back in London attending an ophthalmic outpatient clinic. Thankfully, particularly in view of her childhood blindness, the specialist declared that her eyes would recover completely given some time and a brief course of treatment. Odette, however, believed that her lack of co-ordination, dubious levels of stamina and poor physical strength had let the side down. Indeed, there were many times when she questioned her physical attributes and wondered whether they were up to the task. Her comrades seemed to be far more competent in this area. Recruits were informed that they could leave the school or decline to accept their missions at any point during training, but very few did so. Although Odette was tormented by self-doubt, she did not consider the possibility of opting out, not even for a moment:

There was never any pressure but the training made me all the more determined to do what I could. Not because I was marvellous in any way, but because I knew more about what was happening to people in Europe. There were some English agents who had been captured but had managed to find their way back to England, and they told such dreadful tales about what was happening to certain people. Dreadful stories about what had happened to their friends; so you had a good idea what could happen to you if you were caught. You knew enough to make up your mind about whether you wanted to go into the field or not. The only confidence I had, was that I was confident in myself – not to do a marvellous job or marvellous physical things, but I knew that I could endure a lot. What you don't know is what you will do when you are up against the wall, when you are put to the test. I had an instinct that things could go wrong.[5]

Some time after her training was completed, Odette had made her way through the autumn sunshine to Portman Square to meet with her mentor Buckmaster. The latter was sitting in an easy chair reading her file as she entered his office. He rose quickly and pulled out another easy chair for Odette. Although his eyes took in the swelling and bruising on her face, he made no mention of it whatsoever, he spoke only of her future mission in France.

However, it seems that Buckmaster was confronted with a tricky situation. At the end of the training course the instructors had compiled individual reports for each recruit. These contained detailed character assessments, since in part the training was designed to highlight the positive and negative features of all recruits. While Odette had been worried about her physical weaknesses, the report was more concerned about her character weaknesses. Despite her enthusiastic approach to training Odette's character assessment had not measured up to standards as well as Buckmaster had hoped. The nuns at her earlier convent school had accurately observed her positive and negative character traits and these had not changed one iota with the passage of time. Thus, the SOE training school report dated 25 August 1942 had picked up on her enthusiasm, intelligence and patriotism, but concluded that Odette was too impulsive and stubborn for subversive work.

This official indictment was a severe blow to Buckmaster's plans. French Section was desperately in need of couriers, and he also wanted Odette to establish an entirely new Resistance circuit. Confronted with the training school report, however, he was forced to decide Odette's fate based on his own instinct. With her suitability as an agent seriously under threat Odette and Buckmaster talked for a considerable time that autumn afternoon. It cannot be ascertained for certain whether Buckmaster's final decision was based on the dire shortage of SOE members for the French Section, or from a standpoint of personal confidence in Odette's character and ability to undertake the work. He was not a man to make decisions lightly, but he did appear to have total faith in his own judgement, and by the end of the afternoon he was making plans for Odette's transportation to France.

Notes

1 Imperial War Museum, oral history interview with Odette Hallowes, 1985.
2 Rigden, D., *SOE Syllabus: Lessons in Ungentlemanly Warfare* (Richmond, 2004), pp. 43–45.
3 *Ibid.*
4 Imperial War Museum, oral history interview with Odette Hallowes, 1985.
5 *Ibid.*

5

OPERATION CLOTHIER

Since her career as an agent had hung in the balance while Buckmaster considered her fate that autumn afternoon, Odette was perhaps more grateful than most to accept her undercover assignment, and she was henceforth known and referred to as agent S.23 Lise Clothier within the confines of SOE headquarters. This was the name that she needed to use in all her cipher messages in order to protect her true identity. However, in the field, she initially assumed the name of Odette Metayer for the purposes of working with other agents and French Resistance workers.

The process of smuggling Odette into enemy-occupied territory was known as Operation Clothier. This process involved not only a perilous journey to France and a remit to establish a new Resistance circuit, but also the embracing of a new persona with a fabricated personal history. From years of trial and error, intelligence officers had deduced that an agent's cover story was most effective when it contained some aspects of an agent's real life. Thus, SOE officers had constructed a new life story for Odette which cleverly integrated fact and fiction. In the constructed identity, Odette was to play the role of a French widow whose husband Jean Metayer had died of bronchitis during the bitter winter of 1936. Her educational history was kept intact but there were a few clever diversions from the truth in relation to a number of other areas of her life. New names, addresses and dates needed to be committed to memory, and she was given a new wedding ring that was engraved with the date of her fictitious marriage. Before leaving for France Odette was required to recite repeatedly her new history to intelligence officers until she was word perfect. They questioned and probed her constantly about her new identity in an attempt to detect some flaws in its construction. But Odette was not fazed by these interrogations and gave a perfect and sincere rendition of her new character, even to the point of feigning tears when talking of her fictional husband's untimely death.

Odette's new fabricated life history was backed up by false identity papers and ration cards. Final preparations before going into the field included a detailed checklist of her person and her belongings. No longer would she be able to display finely manicured and varnished nails since, as a quiet widow making her living as a seamstress, her hands had to be well-worn and needle pricked, with an indentation on her left thumb from years of wearing a thimble. Her grey flannel suit was fitted with French clothing labels. In her suitcase subdued lilac and pale blue blouses were folded, French style, alongside some loose fitting trousers, pullovers and underwear. Her face was scrubbed clear of make-up and her dark brown hair was pulled back from her face and tied severely with a black ribbon, a token of mourning for her late husband.

Some personal effects were necessary, because the absence of these always aroused suspicion. A small constructed family photograph was fixed securely in a delicate French picture frame and placed amidst her clothes. Hair brushes, combs, a hand mirror, soap, a simple red lipstick and face powder all bore the hallmarks of reasonably priced French beauty shops. A French torch, compass and map were tucked into her case for good measure. As she observed her neatly packed suitcase crammed with her new belongings, an SOE official handed her a small packet that contained her suicide pill, a grim reminder of her dangerous occupation. With a brief nod in his direction she placed it quickly in her handbag. Along with her official orders she was also given the sum of 500 francs.

At the SOE briefing station, Odette had been lectured about how she should behave in accordance with her new identity. She was not allowed to act in a flirtatious manner, nor draw attention to herself at any time. A good agent needed to remain inconspicuous, unassuming and observant of others. Her accent needed to be that of an ordinary working woman and not that of a sophisticated lady. Her walk, her mannerisms, eating habits, handwriting and general demeanour all needed to conform to her new persona. She needed to be vigilant at all times and not let her guard slip in any respect. There was a lot of information to consider and remember.

The original transportation plan revolved around sending Odette to France by submarine, but as Odette recalled:

> The submarine commanders said they had never had a woman on one of their submarines and they never would – so that was that.[1]

Totally rejected by the Royal Navy, SOE officials cautiously approached the Royal Air Force, since their officers were considered to be more liberal-minded about such matters. The RAF duly consented and the parties concerned waited and prepared for inclement weather. Eventually, when Operation Clothier was about to be implemented, Odette prepared for take-off.

Unfortunately, her journey to France was nowhere near as straightforward as Odette would have liked. The first attempt at take-off was by Whitley bomber from Bristol airport. This attempt failed dramatically when an incoming aircraft collided with the Whitley as it taxied along the runway. Everyone was naturally a bit shaken by the experience but all escaped uninjured.

Following this minor disaster the SOE tried to transport Odette to France by Lysander aircraft; but just as they were preparing for take-off, breaking news came across the radio, informing the crew that her prospective hosts had been captured by the Gestapo and executed. The third attempt by seaplane was thwarted by atrocious weather and the fourth nearly killed her, because the Whitley suffered engine failure just after take-off. It crashed in pitch-black darkness, dangerously close to a cliff edge, with an enormous thud. Pilot and crew were forced to evacuate the aircraft rapidly and run for their lives in case it caught fire. Odette was beginning to think that she was well and truly jinxed following this series of somewhat dramatic false starts.

> Every time I got on a plane [laughs] something went wrong with it, and I was costing them a lot of money.[2]

In the meantime, Buckmaster had decided that as far as Odette was concerned, it was probably better to abandon the prospect of air travel altogether. So he made arrangements for Odette to be transported by cramped troopship across to the forbidding Rock of Gibraltar to await the arrival of a felucca that would take her to France.

The crossing to Gibraltar was particularly rough since the ship was overwhelmed by early winter fog and horizontal rain. It was not the quickest way to travel, but at least Odette had begun her journey. She was also encouraged by the spirit of optimism that pervaded the ship, a contagious level of cheerfulness that was fuelled by Field Marshal Montgomery's recent victories in North Africa. The battle for control of the seas had also shifted in the Allies' favour, because the use of radar and accurate intelligence information had reduced the number of British naval losses. It was abundantly clear that the war was entering a new phase and the Allies were expressing a buoyant, almost palpable confidence.

On her arrival in Gibraltar Odette made her way to a small hotel, and once in her tiny room, with a view of the sea, she unpacked her small brown leather suitcase. As she awaited the imminent arrival of the felucca, and in between unsettled bouts of sleep, Odette felt a profound sense of pride. At long last, she was about to be given the opportunity of playing her own small part in the defeat of Nazi Germany.

The following day a young, tawny-skinned fisherman named Jan arrived at her billet. But when he first set eyes on Odette he threw his arms up into the air in horror. During his security briefing he had only been given Odette's code number and was utterly dumbfounded to discover that he was expected to transport women in his little fishing boat. He had very fixed ideas about womanhood and the role of women. Undaunted by his enraged outbursts, Odette invited the bad-tempered Polish fisherman over to the bar where she plied him with good quality whisky. In a calm and detached manner she explained in great detail the lengths she had already gone to in an effort to begin her mission. He sat with her for some time, enraptured by her soft accent and determined spirit. Once she had completed the story of her misadventures to date she gently convinced him that she could be extremely useful on board his dirty little fishing boat. There followed a lengthy exchange of words, some heated, some low and soft. But it was testimony to Odette's powers of persuasion that when the felucca eventually left Gibraltar later that afternoon Odette and her colleagues were on board. Laughingly, Odette recalled her arguments with Jan:

> He was a very brave man to travel all that way to France in a small fishing boat. I was refused by the navy, they said they'd never had a woman aboard their vessels and never would! I told Jan that I could be useful aboard his boat and offered to do his cleaning.[3]

Jan's small boat was crammed with agents and weapons, all destined for different parts of France. There was also a variety of flags on board, one to suit all occasions. These enabled the felucca to claim allegiance to any nation at a moment's notice. The turbulent October waters tossed the cargo hither and thither, and most of the passengers were seasick by the second day. At one point the small boat sank so low in the water that fish came onto the deck, flapping and slithering as they frantically tried to return to the water. Luckily Odette was not prone to travel sickness of any kind. In fact, the rougher the sea became, the more exhilarated she began to feel. The bitterly cold, foaming spray that periodically threatened to overwhelm the ship only served to blow away the cobwebs from her mind. Besides, she had given her word to Jan that she would be useful aboard his vessel and she was as good as her word. By the third day at sea she had worked through a backlog of washing up, cleaned the galley until it was spotless and had begun sweeping and mopping the deck.

Through the subsequent days Jan and Odette developed a lively relationship that was sustained by a mutual respect and some witty, goading banter. They played cards, told each other jokes and shared permissible confidences. She discovered that he had lost his entire family and all of his property when the Germans invaded Poland. He frequently drowned his sorrows with whisky, and fervently hoped that at some point in the future he would be given the chance to kill at least a few Germans. A direct opportunity had not yet arisen, but he consoled himself with the notion that he would bring about their downfall indirectly, by ferrying agents and weapons across to France. His brooding brown eyes lit up like a fire when he talked of how he would take his revenge, and how he plotted and schemed by day and night. Even as he steered his ship through the roughest of seas, Jan was consumed by a passionate hatred of those who had robbed him of his loved ones. Not surprisingly, therefore, he commanded his vessel with the bravado of one who had nothing to lose.

On the evening of the eighth day the felucca slid silently into a small craggy bay near Cassis and dropped anchor. The passengers were met by the leader of the Marseille group of Resistance fighters, a tall, lean, enthusiastic man named Marsac. He briefly shook hands with Jan, exchanged a few words and gave him a bottle of whisky. Jan smiled in acknowledgement and gratefully hid the black market alcohol in his galley. Passengers and cargo were offloaded efficiently and quietly. Odette quickly waved farewell to Jan.

Throughout the rough journey from Gibraltar Odette had felt a sense of foreboding. But as she disembarked from what had been a very grimy felucca and was now, thanks to her efforts, sparkling clean, she experienced a strange feeling of detachment. It was as though she were in a dream world. There was something surreal that infused her surroundings and situation. Perhaps it was simply the growing sense of her new and false identity. Subdued voices called her name and she climbed across the jagged wet rocks carrying her small suitcase. Eventually, as she reached some level, firm, mossy ground, she paused and observed the scenery. Dusk was giving way to nightfall and stars were abundant in the clear, moonlit sky above her. Odette had arrived in her beloved homeland at long last and offered up a silent prayer of thanks. She vowed to do everything in her power to reclaim her country from those who had ruthlessly invaded its soil and inflicted their rule upon its people. Despite her exhaustion, and the presence of imminent danger, Odette felt an overwhelming sense of euphoria as she boarded a train with four other agents bound for Cannes. This feeling did not last long. Odette's SOE personnel files record her first impressions:

> I arrived in France the night of 2nd November. I went by Felucca from Gibraltar with Captain Young, Urbain, Madame Lechene, Miss Herbert and Starr. My instructions were to go to Auxerre, find a safe house there and start up a circuit. I was to meet Raoul in CANNES and he was to give me a contact in Paris. We went to Cassis near Marseille and there I met some French people from the CARTE organisation – Dr Bernard and Louis. We only stayed two or

three hours at Cassis and then went on to Cannes. There was an Italian in the party who left us at Cassis. We had all been given the address of the Villa Augusta Cannes in London and there we met Raoul about 1130 am on the 3rd of November. Miss Herbert, Madame Lechene and I all stayed at the Villa Augusta and the men i.e. Urbain and Starr stayed with Baron De Malval at the villa Isabelle. My instructions were that Raoul with the help of CARTE would get me through the demarcation line. Raoul got in touch with CARTE who was no help at all. He said that until he got a message from London he would not do anything; in fact he was almost rude to me. I told Raoul that I did not want to stay about doing nothing and suggested that I should help him, to which he agreed.[4]

Odette had managed to get to France and report to her supervisor Captain Peter Churchill, alias Raoul, but Operation Clothier was already in trouble. Aside from the geographical and logistical problems that were preventing her from reaching her final destination, Odette became aware that some members of the Resistance groups were not particularly security minded.

I never wanted to stay in Cannes, but I could not get to where I was supposed to go. I was supposed to start my own circuit in Auxerre but just after I arrived the South of France was flooded with Italians and it was difficult to get the papers I needed. Certainly Raoul had done a lot of groundwork and he had built a large circuit, but I felt that it was too big.

I felt all the time, that if I could be more on my own then I would last as long as necessary. At that time I wasn't in a position to be suspicious about it, but there were certain people I did not like or trust.[5]

These early reservations were well founded. Raoul had established a large circuit named the Spindle network from his base in Cannes and was doing his best to work in co-operation with a native Resistance group headed by CARTE. This was not an easy task. An intelligence officer reported to SOE headquarters on 19 February 1942 that:

Most Frenchmen cannot bear to be in the wrong and they still blame Britain for their defeat. The more sensible and thinking Frenchmen are pro-British. The French resisting groups are saying 'Help us now and when it is over, leave us to our own salvation'. They consider as their chief enemies those Frenchmen who have allowed themselves to be bullied by the Germans and who have been drawn into the net of 'SYNARCHISME' such as the Worms group, Borotra, Chevalier and many others. They consider themselves technicians and their role to order France for the profit of Germany. In fact, they have become Germanised.[6]

All SOE agents needed to recognise those Frenchmen who were true patriots, those who were potential or existing collaborators and those who were simply disgruntled. This process was not easy.

By 29 July several further reports had confirmed that the CARTE organisation was unreliable.[7] By 3 November, when Odette arrived in Cannes, French Resistance groups were involved in an ongoing and bitter struggle for overall superiority. Furthermore, security breaches were commonplace. Odette had no escape route that would enable her to establish her own circuit in Auxerre; and had very little choice but to stay and assist her supervisor in Cannes. Faced with these difficult and entirely unforeseen circumstances, Raoul contacted SOE headquarters through his radio operator Arnaud, and obtained permission to keep Odette at his side. He rightly believed that Odette would be extremely useful to his own undercover network.

Notes

1 Imperial War Museum, oral history interview with Odette Hallowes, 1985.
2 *Ibid.*
3 *Ibid.*
4 The National Archives: SOE personnel files: Captain Peter Churchill, volume 1, ref: HS9/314.
5 Imperial War Museum, oral history interview with Odette Hallowes, 1985.
6 The National Archives: SOE personnel files: Captain Peter Churchill, 1985.
7 *Ibid.*

6

CANNES AND THE SPINDLE NETWORK

From the outset there was an affinity between Odette and her supervisor in the field, Captain Peter Morland Churchill, alias Raoul. He had previously adopted several pseudonyms; among them Pierre Chove, Chambrun and Chauvet. This was common practice among all undercover agents, but when working with Odette he was consistently known and referred to as Raoul. Furthermore, the instant rapport he established with Odette was not surprising given his confident, flamboyant character and her vivacious, impulsive nature. Peter Churchill's personnel file confirmed that he was an extremely self-assured, decisive and intelligent man. He was fluent in French, Spanish, Italian and German. Educated at the University of Cambridge and captain of the ice hockey team he had also been an international player and obtained fifteen caps. With a tall frame, olive complexion, brown eyes and dark hair, he possessed an abnormally powerful physique. His only defect was poor eye sight, which gave him a problem when reading compass bearings.[1]

During his time in Cannes Raoul had established a large, and at times cumbersome, Resistance circuit known as the 'Spindle' network. But the threads of this network had become tangled and frayed in certain areas over the past few months. He was always on his guard, but gave the appearance of being simply a casual observer of everyday life. Mornings were usually spent sitting by pavement cafés listening to the small talk of the townsfolk of Cannes. Evenings were spent in a discreet restaurant, because one waiter had the very useful habit of sitting and gossiping about local people and events. It was surprising how much information could be gleaned from such regular and seemingly innocent encounters; some were useful and some irrelevant, but this was not for Raoul to decide. SOE members in London sifted through his detailed reports that were written and sent daily via his trusted radio operator Arnaud. His nights were spent locating landing sites for RAF supplies, in meetings and planning sabotage operations with Resistance fighters, distributing funds, finding safe houses for agents who were on the run and ferrying messages to Arnaud. His official remit was:

> To be senior British Liaison officer to British personnel in zones between the South East Mediterranean coast and the line Paris–Nancy. To be primarily responsible for the circuit Haute Savoie, to give guidance to all our organisers in these zones concerning local problems; seeing that they keep within the limits of these zones; to ensure the equitable distribution of funds between them; to organise an inter-circuit courier service, and to supervise the provision of dropping grounds, post boxes and safe houses for each zone.[2]

Raoul's attention, for the most part, was focused on gathering intelligence, curbing the enthusiasm of French patriots and remaining one step ahead of his enemies.

The latter could essentially be divided into two distinct groups: the Vichy police and the Gestapo. The official French police were employed and directed by the Vichy government. They were collaborators, detested by all patriots. Most of the time Raoul viewed the Vichy police with extreme contempt. In his opinion they looked ridiculous. They tended to be stunted men, and the little capes that formed part of their uniform conspired to make them look even shorter. Their daily work appeared to consist of blowing loudly on their pathetically shrill whistles and waving their arms frantically at traffic. They could not be underestimated however, because they worked hand in hand with the Gestapo. While they focused on directing traffic and checking paperwork, they could, and often did, report any petty crime to the Gestapo. Many a Resistance worker had fallen foul of their pedantic paperwork and sycophantic desire to please the enemy. Therefore, it was as well to avoid them as much as possible.

The Gestapo were in a different league. They did not wear uniforms, but mingled with ordinary people in train stations, busy streets and cafés. They could be anywhere at any time. They had an unnerving habit of suddenly collecting all young, fit-looking members of a given town's population and sending them to labour camps to assist the German war effort. This practice had not been inflicted on Cannes to date but the Gestapo's reputation preceded them. They were elusive, steely and grey creatures who operated all along the 'unoccupied' (Vichy) coastline.

SOE lectures had pointed out to all agents that the reputation of the Gestapo had been built on ruthlessness and terror, not on intelligence.[3] But in Raoul's game the enemy was not always a known entity. Indeed, the enemy could emerge at any time from within his own ranks. Even those who were supposedly his trusted friends were not particularly security-conscious. He knew of several men who had betrayed their closest friends to the Gestapo for a few francs. It was wise to be careful and alert at all times.

At the point when Odette joined Raoul's team there were two main undercover organisations working in France. The first of these consisted of French patriot groups who operated in the south. The largest of these was known as the COMBAT network. The second organisation consisted of a number of independent sabotage groups that operated over a wider geographical area. In theory, the Frenchmen working within these latter groups remained, at all times, under the command of British officers. Both organisations depended on the same British radio operator in order to maintain direct contact with London, but they did not have any contact with each other. Raoul was required to know and understand the intricate workings of both organisations but often found it difficult to maintain a level of professional detachment when dealing with rival groups. Disputes emerged on a frequent basis as Resistance leaders vied for membership support.

The roots of the Spindle network lay in the foothills of the French Alps. It was here that young, fit Frenchmen would hide out to avoid being forced into Nazi labour camps. These patriots were eager to reclaim their country but could be exuberant to the point of recklessness. Raoul aimed to keep them subdued until the time was ripe for an Allied invasion, and supplied them with information, arms, sabotage equipment, food, clothing and money. He was also responsible for training their members in sabotage techniques. In addition, his remit was to gain the plans and details of individual French ports. This information was vital to the British War Office in the build-up to the D-Day landings. His file records the order of importance of ports and instructions as follows:

> Marseilles.
> Port de Bouc/Etang de Berre.
> Sete.
> Port St Louis de Rhone.
> In case of danger of German or Italian seizure of French shipping in Mediterranean, please deal with this shipping as follows:
> Whenever possible direct ships to allied ports.
> Sink or immobilise others.
> Whenever possible block harbour by sinking of ships in fairway. At Caronte and Marseilles destroy swing bridges, if possible, as this would have the effect of blocking the harbour.[4]

In many respects Odette was a Godsend to Raoul's operation. She was eager, bright and quick to learn. Moreover, in arguments and debates she had a certain feminine charm that easily won over some of the more difficult members of his group. There were times when Raoul was frustrated and kept on a tight rein. He had planned several sabotage attacks for nearby bridges and factories that he had wanted to stage soon after Odette's arrival. He had identified potential targets and wanted to implement the operations because he believed that his men needed to practise their sabotage techniques. They were prone to restlessness if they had no objective. But orders came through from London which clearly stated that all sabotage efforts needed to be restricted to the 'occupied zone'. Reluctantly, therefore, his legitimate targets were promptly abandoned and replaced by 'mock exercises' that could be held in remote fields.

Every day, as he passed the swish hotels and tall town houses of the Croisette, Raoul would think about the numerous tasks that lay ahead. He would push his bicycle down the little side alley that led to his cramped but strategically positioned flat, and prop it up against the wall with its peeling paintwork and crumbling exterior. He was used to dealing with difficult circumstances. His second in command had been captured and shot by the Gestapo, one of the expected deliveries of Bren guns had failed to arrive, he had had to find three 'bolt holes' in less than twenty-four hours for agents 'on the run', and more recently, internal feuds and petty jealousies were threatening to destabilise a French undercover group led by the French patriot Renard. It was entirely likely that Renard's days as their leader were numbered.

But this was the least of Raoul's problems. A number of radio sets and Bren guns were expected by air and he had lost a lot of sleep searching for appropriate landing sites. Storage was problematic because two of the cellars currently in use were stocked to the brim with weapons, food and cigarettes. Another was overflowing with contraband petrol. There was a large cellar at the bakery, but this had recently aroused suspicion after the baker's wife had been rather talkative in the wrong quarters. The steady flow of new agents by boat compounded his logistical problems, since they also had to be housed and located appropriately. Most evenings after his café dinner he would feel distinctly weary as he prepared for the aerial drops of arms and supplies. Luckily he was blessed with stamina and fortitude. As a longstanding friend noted of his character:

He was an idealist, but a very practical matter of fact idealist, never entering on an assignment until he could see the practical steps which he would have to take to carry it out successfully. From the point of view of an organiser of underground activities in enemy-occupied territory, he was a 'natural'. His French was perfect, he was quick to grasp the complexities of a problem, and, above all, he had an intuitive sense of responsibility and initiative.[5]

Despite his natural talent for organising subversive activity, Raoul was unable to fully supervise and control the independent Resistance groups. Security was poor and from time to time some of the groups were infiltrated by German spies. These spies usually emanated from the German intelligence organisation Abwehr. The resulting fallout when underground networks were exposed could be catastrophic in terms of the overall movement. All agents, therefore, ran a daily risk of capture, torture and execution. This situation kept most agents on their guard and Raoul approached each new mission with extreme caution, knowing that one false move could endanger not only his life but also the lives of others under his command.

Odette, meanwhile, was adapting to the role of under-cover agent with a certain ease, despite missing her children terribly. She did experience periods of agitation; life in Cannes was not quite what she had expected. Having left behind the desperate austerity of wartime Britain she was shocked by the number of luxury goods that were so readily available on the black market in southern France. She also despised the glamorous, empty-headed wives of Vichy officials who flaunted their wealth and prestige by attending their hair and beauty salons as though nothing untoward was happening around them. It was like another world entirely, and as a native French woman she despaired at the shame of Vichy France. Cannes still boasted an array of beautiful, elegant houses and quaint, expensive shops. The Mediterranean sun still shone with some intensity in the early winter mornings, and the people calmly went about their business, seemingly oblivious to the overriding tyranny that had swept across Europe.

Odette's initial view of intelligence work was that it required a lot of hanging around in dubious places, and making arrangements to meet with even more dubious characters. She firmly believed that she would have been more use in northern France where her patriots were suffering, rather than in the south surrounded by what she referred to as 'Vichy poodles'. A naturally impatient and impulsive character, Odette was always happier when she could be involved in some direct action. There was something of the commando in her personality that she found difficult to suppress.

Since her arrival Odette had worked primarily as a courier, and this was a dangerous occupation. Amongst other things it involved the gathering and delivering of crucial intelligence information to and from undercover Resistance workers. Sometimes she would travel great distances, usually by bicycle, in order to collect plans, maps, grid references and timetables for agent arrivals and parachute drops. This particular aspect of her work represented a personal triumph for Odette because, up until this point in her life, she had never actually ridden a bicycle. Raoul only discovered this fact when her steep learning curve involved a tumble into a hedgerow followed by grazed and muddy knees and a torn skirt. But over the following weeks she became adept at cycling down small and obscure country lanes, and would often approach them at breakneck speed.

In addition to her courier work, Odette helped Raoul to measure prospective landing sites in advance of RAF drops, assisted in the acquisition of safe houses and provided him with invaluable knowledge of her native country. All their intelligence work, however, relied on the skills and loyalty of their radio operator. Without him and his reliable radio set, no information could reach SOE headquarters. Their current radio operator, Arnaud, had recently taken over from a British operator named Julien, who had been on the verge of mental and physical exhaustion.

Arnaud, whose real name was Lieutenant Adolfe Rabinovitch, was an extremely loyal member of the group and an excellent and dependable radio operator. He was a tall, broad-shouldered, handsome man with dark hair and deep brown eyes, who usually dressed in casual clothes and a grubby weatherbeaten mackintosh. Renowned for being abrupt, emotionally labile, prone to violence, humourless and extremely bad-tempered, he also swore a great deal. But together, throughout the following weeks, the angry Arnaud, suave Raoul and the quick-witted Odette forged an interesting and somewhat unlikely triangle of deep and loyal comradeship. Odette's personnel file recorded:

Arnaud was an extremely difficult character and was difficult to get along with, but he was a very brave man and the best at his job in France. Apart from his work he was impossible, and Raoul was the only person who could get along with him. Arnaud also liked Odette very much and when Raoul was not there he would only work with her. Odette said that she always felt perfectly sure of Arnaud and that he would die for her if necessary. She said that the three of them, Raoul, Arnaud and Odette formed a perfect team and could trust one another completely, and would readily lay down their lives for one another.[6]

Notes

1   The National Archives: SOE personnel files: Captain Peter Churchill, volume 2, ref: HS9/315.
2   *Ibid.*
3   Rigden, D., *SOE Syllabus: Lessons in Ungentlemanly Warfare* (Richmond, 2004), p. 85.
4   The National Archives: SOE personnel files: Captain Peter Churchill, volume 1, ref: HS9/314.
5   *The Times*, 2 May 1972, Captain Peter Churchill Obituary, p. 16.
6   The National Archives: SOE personnel files: Odette Sansom, ref: HS9/648/4.

MARSEILLE

Odette had only been on home territory for four days before setting off on her first mission alone. A mixture of impatience and obstinacy succeeded in convincing Raoul that she was ready to go it alone.

> About 6th November he sent me off on a mission to Marseille where I had to contact Gilles and Gisele and to take them a message from Raoul. I was also supposed to contact Marsac and Muriel and bring back a case to Cannes for Raoul. We could not find this case for a long time and I stayed in Marseille for one night. All this time I was living with Raoul at the villa Augusta and we were working as man and wife.[1]

Marseille had been viciously bombed in 1940 and little was left of the quaint old quarter of the town. The place was also teeming with German soldiers and on her arrival at the train station Odette was confronted by one for the first time. Mentally she noted his rank and looked him up and down curiously as she mingled with the station crowd. Much to her own surprise she realised that she was looking for signs of racial superiority. After some time, she concluded that his young pasty-looking face, distinctly podgy belly and stocky, sweaty frame bore little resemblance to the German propaganda films of fit musclebound youths marching in joyful unison to the solemn tones of Wagner. Dressed in her charcoal-grey flannel suit with a discreet lilac blouse Odette presented her forged papers with a new air of confidence as she left the station to find Gilles and Gisele. It was around eleven thirty in the morning. Following her instructions to the letter she proceeded to find the small and somewhat chaotic garage where two mechanics were busy changing tyres and checking the oil of a bus that had clearly seen better days. So far so good; once the necessary passwords had been exchanged Raoul's message was delivered without a hitch, and she had only to wait until six o'clock in the evening in order to meet with Marsac and Muriel. In her smart black handbag Odette was carrying a large amount of money wrapped in a rather tatty brown envelope. This money was for Marsac. He was the leader of the Marseille Resistance group and needed these funds to maintain the effectiveness of his work.

Not wanting to wander the streets all afternoon with the risk of drawing attention from the Gestapo, Odette chose to visit the cinema. There she waited all afternoon watching seemingly endless German propaganda films. The cinema lights were not dimmed during screenings, since the Nazis had discovered that if they dimmed the lights there were always catcalls and yells of abuse from the predominantly French audience. Subsequently, as the propaganda films were shown with the lights full on, German soldiers scanned the audience intently for signs of dissent. Being in a French cinema at this point was a somewhat surreal process, therefore, since the audience sat like motionless zombies, afraid to react to any image presented in front of them.

Later that afternoon, having had her fill of German propaganda, Odette walked briskly through the streets of Marseille, stopping occasionally to read the official notices that were posted on every corner. Some of these were even posted in shop windows but Odette was heartened by their content. They were testimony to the fact that German authorities were becoming increasingly worried about the activities of the French population. The most recent notice read:

Il est interdit de dissimmuler aux recherches, d'heberger ou d'aider d'une autre facon dés personnes appurtenant a une force armee ennemie (notamment dés members d'equipages d'avions, ou dés parachutists ennemis, ou dés agents enemies).[2]

[It is forbidden to conceal, befriend or aid in any way persons who are part of the Army of the enemy (particularly members of air crew, enemy parachutists and enemy agents).]

The notice also included dire warnings to the French population about the potential consequences of giving aid to the enemy, pointing out that:

Whoever contravenes the above order exposes themselves to being brought before a military tribunal and there they will be punished with the utmost severity, in some cases the pain of death.[3]

However, the Nazis adopted a 'carrot and stick' approach to Resistance activities and were not averse to bribing members of the population. The warning notice concluded by offering a reward to anyone who was willing to come forward and give them precise information with regard to parachute landings and the whereabouts of enemy airmen:

> Whoever declares openly the discovery of an airman who has made a forced landing and cites the day, time and exact location of the landing, or presents irrefutable evidence of an airman's body or parachute will be rewarded. Reward will be on the assurance of military personnel or where any enemy agent's admission has aided his capture.[4]

The very fact that the Nazis had deemed it necessary to warn the population gave credibility to the progress and growing effectiveness of the Resistance movement. In her current state of naivety Odette did not contemplate, nor dwell on the possibility, that one Frenchman might betray another for something as distasteful as monetary reward. Her own sense of honour and duty frequently blinded her to the lack of honour in others. Odette's integrity had a quality of childlike innocence, and her initial inability to detect the true nature of some of her compatriots reflected an alarming lack of worldly experience. She simply did not understand the Vichy collaborators; in her eyes these people were clearly not French at all. She viewed them as spoilt rich people who had no patriotism and perhaps no bloodline of any note. For her, it was impossible to conceive of a situation whereby French men and women would side with the enemy and give them information. Then, as she slowly turned a corner, she noticed poster images of German soldiers. They glared out at her with steely eyes, brandishing guns from nearby buildings that had almost been reduced to rubble. Hanging some distance away from the grave curfew notices a series of recruitment posters adorned the bombed-out buildings.

With a growing sense of outrage and disbelief Odette realised that the Germans were attempting to recruit Frenchmen into the Waffen SS. Indignantly she turned her back on the offending posters and hurried along the busy streets towards her destination.

At six o'clock precisely she met Marsac and Muriel at a small café near the train station. The rendezvous was chosen primarily so that Odette could make the exchange and almost immediately climb aboard her return train to Cannes. But Marsac had encountered a problem. For some bizarre reason, he had been unable to locate the case that contained, among other things, plans of the port of Marseille. Odette began to feel nervous and declared that she was not prepared to hand over large sums of money without first obtaining the case. The small group returned to Marsac's apartment and began to search for the missing case. Two hours later, the case was located among some rubbish and books in an understairs cupboard. Odette heaved a sigh of relief before suddenly remembering another problem. Clearly she was now unable to catch her return train as planned. More importantly, there was a nine o'clock curfew on the streets of Marseille. Anyone caught walking around after this time was instantly arrested and interrogated by the dreaded Gestapo.

There followed a heated discussion before Marsac contacted another Resistance member for advice, then he hurriedly wrote an address on a piece of paper and pressed it into the dainty hand of Odette. He explained that the address he had given her was not the most salubrious in terms of accommodation but he assured her that she would be safe. Odette's earlier confidence had now dissipated and she made her way nervously to what she hoped would be her bolt hole. Several times she was convinced that she was being followed, and she hid in poorly lit doorways whenever she heard jackboots.

Forty-five minutes later, a tense Odette was knocking earnestly on the door of a notorious backstreet brothel, one frequented by German soldiers. It seemed like an eternity before the madam opened the door, and the heavily painted elderly woman observed Odette with a mixture of amusement and suspicion, before noticing her intensely fearful expression. Once she realised that Odette was actually looking for sanctuary rather than applying for a job at her establishment, she beckoned her up some rickety wooden stairs and into a shabby second-floor room. Uttering words of assurance, followed by instructions to keep her door locked at all times, the madam left Odette with the precious case and proceeded to descend the staircase to attend to her customers.

The sounds of the brothel ensured that the anxious Odette did not sleep a wink. Low German male voices mixed with seductive female French tones to make a cocktail of conversational hum that was impossible to understand. Occasionally it was possible for her to make out the odd word, and sometimes the feigned shrill laughter of the prostitutes would pierce her ears and interrupt her thoughts. The room was dirty and smelly. Threadbare carpet was complimented by the grubby torn netting at the window. Cracked glass in the window panes was matched by the cracked glass in a free-standing mirror that stood forlornly in the corner of the room. Although the madam had insisted that she would be safe, Odette had taken no chances. Once in the room, she had locked the door and lugged the moth-eaten mattress across the entrance. Then, she shifted an old dresser and positioned it in front of the mattress and piled two wooden chairs on top of her barricade. Finally, she'd looked calmly out of the window to locate the whereabouts of the drainpipe. It was close enough for her to grab onto and use as an escape route if necessary, though given the building's general state of repair, she was not convinced that the pipe was secure enough to take her weight. Nevertheless, there was little else that could be done to prepare the way for a quick exit and, reasonably satisfied with her room alterations, Odette rested with her eyes half closed in a worn-out easy chair by the door.

At three o'clock in the morning the general hum of conversation and shrill laughter was broken by angry, loud German voices and the heavy clumping of booted footsteps on the staircase. Odette could feel the adrenaline rising in her bloodstream as she got up from her easy chair and listened intently to the angry voices. Apparently a young German soldier had disappeared. He had gone absent without leave. His commanding officer was demanding a search of all buildings, particularly brothels that he was known to have frequented in the past. Odette wondered if she should simply plaster her face with make-up and pretend that she was a prostitute, but decided that there was no time for her to hide the case. For a brief moment she contemplated the prospect of emptying the case and hiding the documents about her person. But she was not entirely sure of the number of documents, and hiding them beneath her clothes might prove to be difficult. She suspected that a map of the port of Marseille lay hidden within the case. Logically, she concluded that this map would be crucial to the Allies. But it was not for her to decide about the remaining documents, she was not sure which documents to save and which to abandon. Following this rapid train of thought Odette decided to leave the case and its belongings intact.

As the brothel madam and the German army search party stopped outside her door Odette held her breath and feared the worst. Then she heard the madam explain in a confident manner, that of course she was happy for the soldiers to enter any room they wished, but she felt it only fair to warn them that in this particular room, one of her girls was very sick with smallpox. None of the other girls would enter the room because the disease was highly contagious; the patient's food and drink, she explained, was always left outside the door as a precaution. But of course, she fully understood their need to search the room so they could go right ahead and open the door. An experienced mistress of the art of deception in all matters, the brothel-keeper knew only too well that there was a limit to German bravado. The German soldiers muttered between themselves for a few moments. Then, just as the madam expected, they decided that they needed no further warning. Grunting some expletives under their breath they turned on their jackboots and retreated down the stairs.

Odette sat back down in the easy chair with immense relief and waited until dawn. As soon as daylight filtered through the cracked window pane, she washed her face with cold water from a brightly coloured jug and mopped it dry with a clean handkerchief retrieved from her handbag. She combed her hair and applied some make-up before cautiously approaching the stairs clutching both her handbag and the case. Eventually, she found the madam drinking acorn coffee in her cluttered kitchen at the back of the house. They exchanged conspiratorial smiles and Odette was ushered out of the building by way of a narrow back alley.

By 11.30 that same morning Odette was back in Cannes and sitting with Raoul at a small café in the sunshine, enjoying a much-needed late breakfast. The case containing the precious documents was safely ensconced in a secret hiding place and her first mission had been successfully accomplished. It was with some satisfaction, therefore, that she recounted her adventure in great detail to Raoul. The latter, however, was not unduly impressed, and warned her gently about the dangers of succumbing to feelings of smugness. He had been in the field far longer than she and knew that overconfidence could signal the death knell of many a good agent.

Odette felt deflated. She had expected at least some praise and recognition for a job well done. Instead, she was met with stern caveats and her behaviour was being scrutinised. Nevertheless, later on that day she noted on reflection, that Raoul observed events from a different perspective than she, and it was at that point Odette realised that she still had a lot to learn.

Notes

1 The National Archives: SOE personnel files: Odette Sansom, ref: HS9/648/4.
2 Imperial War Museum Picture Archive, The French Resistance: German poster reproduced and translated in Album 854.
3 *Ibid.*
4 *Ibid.*

8

RADIO DAYS

The French Resistance movement could only operate effectively if it was adequately supplied with guns, explosives and other sabotage equipment. Members of the movement relied entirely on couriers like Odette to inform them of crucial parachute drops. However, the times and locations of parachute drops were frequently altered at the last minute. Good communication was usually the key to a successful mission but the courier service was dependent on public transport and old fashioned bicycles. Consequently, information was sometimes incorrect by the time it reached its destination. For instance, an agent could cycle thirty miles with vital instructions about aerial deliveries, but these heavily laden aeroplanes could later be grounded due to bad weather. By relying on this cumbersome communication system, agents wasted a lot of time and took unnecessary risks. Furthermore, as networks expanded geographically it became virtually impossible to communicate information quickly.

This problem was eventually resolved by a gentleman named George Noble. As the first French Section agent in the field, he understood these communication difficulties and suggested that the SOE should involve the BBC in their covert operations. It was possible, he argued, for the

BBC to alert interested bodies across the Channel about their deliveries by way of coded, pre-agreed messages. The process was simple, since the BBC already transmitted personal messages at the end of some of their programmes. These were usually messages to members of the armed forces from their loved ones back home. If other more 'loaded' messages were added to these, he suggested, they would not necessarily arouse suspicion. His innovative idea was taken up by Buckmaster, and following some discreet discussions with BBC controllers, the BBC World Service became an integral part of SOE clandestine operations. Subsequently, pre-arranged coded messages were slipped in to the personal message bulletins that were broadcast between 7.30 and 9.15 each night. Through these bulletins the BBC were able to inform SOE agents when a parachute drop was imminent. Romantic and innocent-sounding messages thus became the signal for Resistance groups across Europe to leap into action.

Some Resistance leaders were highly suspicious of this new communication method, however, and argued that it was open to corruption and enemy infiltration. But over a period of time the BBC proved its worth. Indeed, in terms of spreading the news about supply deliveries, a reliance on the radio was a great improvement on the earlier reliance on the bicycle. But no sooner had one problem been resolved than another took its place.

Internal disputes within some Resistance groups were coming to a head. Raoul refused to take sides in these disputes, even though it was clear that internal fighting threatened to wreck some groups entirely. Some leaders were notably power hungry and prone to exaggerate their level of support, as Odette recalled:

Girard was head of a French Resistance group working with Peter Churchill. His men wanted him removed and went to Peter about it. Because it was a domestic matter Peter would not interfere. Girard failed to get a vote of confidence from his men and was sent to England and then to America.[1]

Other Resistance leaders were also a problem from time to time, but it was rare for members to rise up against their leader. Furthermore, this was not the first time that Girard, leader of the CARTE organisation, had presented a problem. The following telegram, sent to SOE headquarters in January 1943, outlined the reasons for the unprecedented level of dissent within the ranks.

Cipher telegram from BERNE
DISPATCHED 1735 HRS 15/1/1943
RECEIVED 2340 HRS 15/1/1943
Inactivity plus Carte's egoism lack of courtesy lack of interest for men in danger or distress caused general feeling of insecurity. He drives too hard, gives too many orders.

Being Carte's small hand man I regret to have to report he has gone off at the deep end. In spite of qualities excellent relations etc: losing followers daily. Hard working courageous, but chiefly unnerved by Carte's temperamental high flying whims and blundering lack of caution.

HERE IS WHY YOU SHOULD REFUSE YOUR SUPPORT TO CARTE:

1. HE GETS NO RESULTS SO DOES NOT NEED ARMS.
2. INCAPABLE OF ORGANISING RECEPTIONS. (ONE PARACHUTE OPERATION IN FIVE MONTHS)

3. INCOMPATIBLE TEMPERAMENT WITH
   ALL YOUR AGENTS HE IS ANTI-BRITISH ONLY
   PRO-CARTE.
4. HE HAS MEANS OF INTERNAL LIAISON WHICH HE
   DOES NOT USE.
5. BAD QUALITIES CAUSING LOSS OF MEMBERS,
   GOOD WILL AND RECRUITS.
6. HE IS UNABLE TO BRING IN PROMISED MILITARY
   PERSONAGES.
7. HIS RADIO TEXTS ARE UNSETTLING AND NOT
   UNDERSTOOD, OFTEN TOO PRECISE THEY
   INCITE GERMAN PRESS.[2]

Despite the fact that Raoul did not take sides with members of the CARTE organisation about its leadership, he had certainly argued with Girard for some months, even before Odette's arrival, about his incompetence and recklessness. Some field operations had been a shambles because of his lack of planning and general disregard for safety. On one memorable occasion he forgot to bring the torches that were necessary to guide the aircraft over the dropping point. Odette had also observed the shoddiness of his work:

At the end of November 1942 it was decided that either Raoul or Carte had to go back to London and a Halifax operation was tried on the ground near Arles. Unfortunately when we got there we found that the ground had been ploughed up, we presumed by the Germans and I should think only the day before. Raoul, Carte, Colonel Vautrin, Jaboum and I all went to the ground and when the plane came over Raoul made a sign to show that we were there but that the operation could not be carried out. Colonel Vautrin walked across the field with Carte and got very cross and excited and they were all very rude and told us plainly that the British were stupid. This ground had been chosen by Carte's people and Raoul had sent it back to London via Arnaud. They got the field through a woman living in the village near Manosque near AIX-EN-PROVENS. This woman had a daughter about 15 who was an idiot. The woman was tall, thin, with fair hair nearly grey and was over 40. Her husband was an officer in the army but not in France. We returned to Cannes after this and went back to work.

About this time the men working for CARTE decided they did not want to work with him any more, and they came to Raoul and said they wanted to work with us and there was nearly a small revolution. Raoul got into touch with London and told them of this difference and we then had special orders to send CARTE to London. We tried the operation again at the end of December in a new field near Arles. I believe this ground was also found by Carte. The plane came but something was wrong with the times and the operation could not be done – I think it was the fault of the R.A.F. this field became brulé [compromised] after Christmas.

We went back to Cannes and things were going very badly with CARTE. His Lieutenant Frager did not want to work with him any more. My opinion of Frager is that I think him a very good man for an army job he is certainly very clever and did not work to achieve glory for himself as did CARTE. Even Carte's own men did not want to work with him any more. I refused to work with him as his security was so bad it was just not safe. Raoul complained about Carte's insecurity and London gave orders that Raoul should come to London and things could be settled. In January we were supposed to make the operation in Tournus. This operation was only for Raoul as by that time we had nothing to do with Carte. He arranged his operation through Gaullists and we knew nothing about it until it had taken place. As things were becoming very difficult Raoul thought he could not possibly leave France so suggested I came to London so I went to TOURNUS with Raoul, Frager, Carte and Roger (BRAY). The latter was a French man from Lyons who was acting as a courier for Frager. He was tall, thin about 26 years old. Raoul was organising this operation. At Tournus the night before we were expecting the operation Raoul said that he would go and look at the field, so he took a bicycle and went off. On the field he was met by some people who asked 'Have you got some potatoes?' He replied that he did not understand and thinking this procedure rather strange he stayed there in a corner of the field. After a time a plane came down and he saw some people come off the plane and others going in. The plane was there for 2½ hours because it got stuck in the mud. By this time of course, everyone in Tournus had heard about this plane so the field was brulé and early next morning the Germans were on the field. This operation was done by the Gaullist organisation and took place about the 18th of Jan. We were then living in Annecy and St Jorioz was our HQ. We moved there just before this operation. The reason we moved was mainly because of Carte's insecurity. He was going about telling people that he would put everyone in jail. Raoul's security was very bad as CARTE and his men were so talkative that many people knew we were staying in the Villa Augusta so it was imperative that we should move. Also there was some trouble with Baron De Malval. He was left in charge of some money and when we asked for it it could not be found. There was some argument and we rather suspected him.[3]

Eventually the organisation's members denounced Girard and opted for a joint leadership formed by the deputy leader Paul Frager and the leader of the Marseille group, Andre Marsac. Ostracised from the main Resistance group Girard decided to form a small breakaway group. This development caused severe problems because Girard already knew all the BBC codes and the dropping areas for the following moon cycle. Parachute drops could only be made in bright moonlight and this restricted the number of drops to a period of six days either side of the full moon. Aircraft also needed certain conditions in order to approach the dropping point. When she was not delivering and collecting messages, therefore, Odette spent most of her daytime hours searching for suitable dropping points. According to the SOE manual, Odette was required to consider the following principles in her everyday search:

Look for an open space not less than six hundred yards square, unless it is anticipated that several containers and/ or men will be dropped, in which case it should be eight hundred yards square. By taking this area the ground would be suitable for any wind direction.

Avoid agricultural ground because of the risk of injury, especially to ankles. Evidence will also be left in the form of tracks and damaged crops. Avoid swamps. Grass parkland is ideal for personnel, but for containers most types of ground will be found suitable.

There should be no high tension wires or telegraph poles in the vicinity. There should be no clumps of trees in the middle of the dropping point. Further, for an aircraft to see the light from five hundred feet the latter should be at least five hundred yards from one hundred foot trees.

If possible, there should be at least one 'safe house' within a mile, but not nearer than a mile, for security reasons.

Allowance must be made for 'wind drift.' It is estimated that there is a sixty yard drift for every five miles per hour increase in the velocity of the wind. This is estimated for a plane flying at the height and speed previously mentioned. No dropping operation should take place if the wind speed is over twenty miles per hour.[4]

Reception committees were on standby throughout the moonlight dropping period, and thanks to the BBC they were able to respond quickly and in a co-ordinated manner. Odette, Raoul and Arnaud would huddle around their radio set each evening waiting for the coded messages that indicated good weather conditions and the arrival of a Lysander or Hudson aircraft. Receiving supplies was an extremely dangerous business and it was vital to dispose of the evidence. Meticulous planning, stealth and speed were key components of a successful mission. Careful instructions to this effect were given to each reception group:

Six men may conveniently handle a container, but it is not necessary to provide that number per container if the men understand their job. Each member of the party should be equipped with gloves as carrying becomes painful owing to the thinness of handles.

If there is a deep lake or river near the dropping point, the container may be conveniently disposed of there. If it is to be buried a suitable burying point should have been chosen beforehand, and if possible holes dug.

Always remember disposal of outer container must be permanent.

In order to ease carrying of cells, a strap or rope may be used to string them on a man's back. In this way one man can carry one cell without much difficulty or fatigue.[5]

Field operations were always risky. Some aircraft were brought down by the Luftwaffe before they reached the dropping point. There were also times when the Nazis managed to discover details about prospective landings and traps were sprung to catch the agents at the last moment. Dogs were frequently used to sniff out the scent of agents and assist in the hunt. Odette had been chased by dogs on three occasions but each time had managed to escape in the nick of time. In the process, however, she did sustain minor ankle and back injuries.

I tripped over one night running down a hill. I ended up sliding the rest of the way down on my back because the ground was so muddy. My back was scraped on rocks and stones and I had twinges of pain for days afterwards.[6]

The aim of all agents who found themselves in this situation was to run to the nearest river or lake to lose their scent, and so shake off the dogs.

Being caught and torn to shreds by dogs was Odette's biggest fear at this time. But the dogs were the least of Raoul's worries. He lived in constant fear of the security breaches that placed everyone in danger. Moreover, in his exile, Girard had acted in a predictable manner, and as soon as parachute drops were made he would turn up with his own band of men and fight with members of the legitimate Resistance group as they grappled with the supplies. Patriotic Frenchmen were now fighting against other patriotic Frenchmen in order to gain supplies. Clearly the situation was becoming farcical. Raoul had placated Girard on several occasions but this ludicrous scenario could not be allowed to continue. The latter frequently claimed that he had hundreds and thousands of followers who were prepared to fight with Allied Command when the need arose. Raoul strongly suspected that this claim was false, and on 26 March 1943 Raoul wrote a letter to SOE headquarters complaining that CARTE was a liar.[7]

At Raoul's request, immediate arrangements were made by the SOE to fly Girard to England. He did not return to the field. Meanwhile, Raoul and Odette continued to live at the Hôtel de la Poste in St Jorioz, which was situated about five miles from the town of Annecy. Over a period of time, and through a series of guarded discussions with the hotel owners, the Cottets, it became clear that another organisation needed SOE help. Raoul was happy to oblige:

> It was through M. Cottet telling me that a large group of organised maquisards were in a certain neighbourhood in March 1943 that I was able to telegraph London and obtain arms and stores for them which were actually delivered by parachute from twenty-five aircraft, five of which were brought down.[8]

Once this arms drop had been arranged, Raoul and CARTE's new joint leader Frager returned to England for strategic talks with Buckmaster. Allied Command were making plans for Operation Overlord and needed to outline the potential role of French Resistance groups within this operation. In the meantime, another British officer named Francis Cammaerts had been sent into the field to make a fresh assessment of the CARTE organisation. Odette, despite her relative inexperience, was left nominally in charge of the circuit in Raoul's absence. Throughout her time in the field Odette had operated as though she were Raoul's wife, since couples generally aroused less suspicion than single agents. In Odette and Raoul's case, they no longer needed to pretend. It was clear to their radio operator Arnaud, and to all who knew them well, that the couple had fallen in love. While this unexpected development made some aspects of their work a lot easier, it also signalled potential danger.

Notes

1   *Daily Telegraph*, 24 November 1958, interview with Odette Hallowes.
2   The National Archives: SOE personnel files: Odette Sansom, ref: HS9/648/4.
3   The National Archives: SOE personnel files: Captain Peter Churchill, volume 1, ref: HS9/314.
4   Rigden, D., *SOE Syllabus: Lessons in Ungentlemanly Warfare* (Richmond, 2004), pp. 146–147.
5   *Ibid.*, p. 150.
6   Imperial War Museum, oral history interview with Odette Hallowes, 1985.
7   The National Archives: SOE personnel files: Captain Peter Churchill, volume 2, ref: HS9/315.
8   *Ibid.*

9

BETRAYAL

In Raoul's absence Odette and Arnaud continued to work as normal. Funds were distributed, parachute drops arranged and safe houses located in much the same way as before. Arnaud had initially resisted the move to the Annecy region because he feared that the nearby mountains would interfere with his radio transmissions. Consequently, some considerable time elapsed before he eventually found suitable accommodation, not far from St Jorioz, above Faverges, in a tiny village named Les Tissots. In order for Odette to communicate with Arnaud, however, it was necessary for her to take a short bus ride into Annecy. They met daily to discuss the state of the war, the problem of waiting for good transmission weather, the routine business of sending reports to London and the merits and drawbacks of dropping points. Both were feeling somewhat relieved since Girard had been removed from the field. Odette in particular was much happier dealing with the new joint leader Marsac. She trusted him implicitly. He had been in Cassis when she first arrived; he had found her much-needed refuge in Marseille, and when her radio had broken it was Marsac who found a replacement. Indeed, Odette was apt to refer to him as the 'ever reliable Marsac'. Couriers came and went but Marsac was ever present, and since Odette had only been working in the field for just over five months she still felt as though she needed some guidance. Although she knew that the British officer Cammaerts had recently arrived from the SOE to make a realistic appraisal of the southern Resistance movements, she saw no reason to seek guidance from him when she could just as easily depend on Marsac. After all, he was one of her native countrymen. For the most part, she believed that she could rely on her own instincts and reasoning. Raoul had placed his trust in her, and he would not have done so if he had harboured any reservations about her capabilities in the field.

By April 1943, some Resistance movements had been infiltrated by Germans and none of those involved with their activities could rely on boundless loyalty. The Abwehr had made substantial inroads and were eager to capture key figures within the Resistance. St Jorioz may have been a small, insignificant village to some, but Raoul had made this village his headquarters. Furthermore, somebody, somewhere had breached security yet again and it was during a routine bus ride to Annecy that Odette first became aware of a tall, smartly dressed gentleman, who appeared to be observing her rather intently through his thick round spectacles.

Up until this point, Odette had been in a buoyant mood. It was a beautiful spring day and she had been gazing out of the bus window at the budding flowers and trees. Shrugging off the man's gaze as she alighted from the bus she continued her business as usual. There were people she needed to meet, observations she needed to make, and shopping she needed to do. Her anxiety levels only began to rise when she realised that the same bespectacled man was also present on her return bus route. On reaching her destination she walked rather more briskly than normal into the hotel reception. As she did so, the man approached her and introduced himself as Henri. He claimed to have important news for her, and some information that may be to her advantage.

They sat and drank acorn coffee as Henri spoke to Odette in quiet measured tones. He told her that he was a German officer with the Abwehr, but one who was disillusioned with the war. He further informed her that Marsac had been arrested while drinking his morning coffee in a small pavement café in the Champs Élysées, Paris, and was now languishing in Fresnes prison. Henri gave Odette a letter from Marsac and coaxingly tried to convince her to travel back with him to Paris to visit him. Odette read the contents of Marsac's letter, which strongly suggested that she should help Henri with his machinations. But perhaps Henri had forced Marsac's hand? Odette smiled and listened patiently to the German officer, but politely refused his invitation. Undeterred by her refusal to accompany him to Paris, Henri continued to speak. He explained that he wanted to go to London to negotiate a peace with the western Allies because he no longer had any faith in any of the Nazi leaders. Not in the least convinced by this tale Odette decided to buy herself some time. She sweetly suggested that she could send a courier to see Marsac and deliver a food parcel. She needed to know for certain that her comrade was safe before she could make a decision. Either way, she assured Henri, she would make contact with London on his behalf and await instructions. It was unlikely, however, that a flight to London could be arranged before 18 April. Henri seemed mollified by her assurances and suggestion and promptly left the hotel with a courier and food.

Feeling distinctly unnerved by her encounter with Henri, Odette immediately retreated to the safety of her

hotel room and wrote a report for Arnaud to transmit to
SOE headquarters. The reply from London was short and
simple. Henri was not to be trusted and Odette was to
take all precautions and wind up the Resistance operation
in St Jorioz. The following morning she travelled into
Annecy and warned as many people as she could about the
impending danger. As a further precaution she insisted on
finding new addresses for Arnaud and Cammaerts, and they
both moved in haste. As a relative newcomer to clandestine
operations Odette genuinely believed that she had acted in
accordance with SOE instructions in every respect. With one
exception, it could be argued that she had indeed followed
instructions to the letter. But Odette was also supposed to
leave the area forthwith, to remain where she was clearly
increased the risk of arrest. Yet instead of abandoning her
position, she stayed in St Jorioz eagerly awaiting the return
of Raoul. This ill-fated action also placed the hotel owners,
the Cottets, in great danger. As Raoul later admitted:

> The Cottets knew who we were but in spite of the risk to
> themselves and their commerce they were of great assistance
> to us, and among the things they did were:
> To allow Lise (Odette) to remain at the hotel when it was
> officially closed.
> They made part of the reception committee which climbed
> the Semnoz, 6000 feet, to receive me when I was parachuted
> on the 15th April 1943.
> Their cellar contained radio parts for four different operators,
> a revolver and quantities of very compromising papers.[1]

Odette firmly believed that the Cottets and Raoul were
safe at this time, because she had told Henri that a flight

to London could not be arranged for him until 18 April. Logically, she did not imagine that he would come searching for her until at least that date. But both Odette and Raoul were culpable of disobeying direct orders. Moreover, it was a mistake that cost them their freedom, and the personnel files of both agents reveal this unpalatable information:

> On arriving in France Spindle [Raoul] stayed the night at the Cottet hotel with Clothier [Odette] instead of, as they had been told to do, going immediately to Glaieuls and they were both arrested by the Gestapo.[2]

In their defence, it can be argued that agents were normally allowed a certain amount of latitude in the field. Raoul was also extremely tired and distressed on his return to St Jorioz because he had just left his dying mother in England. But this was not the time for latitude. During the morning of 16 April Italian troops descended on the hotel. This development alone should have been enough to set alarm bells ringing. In strictly professional terms Raoul was in command, Odette was merely his courier; Raoul was responsible for all strategic decisions and Odette simply obeyed his orders. However, their relationship was no longer strictly professional, and the decision to stay in St Jorioz longer than was necessary was perhaps influenced by the intensity of their feelings for one another rather than common sense.

Subsequently, a myth arose that when Odette and Raoul were arrested they were found in bed together. Yet despite the pervasiveness of this myth it has no basis in fact. While Henri, whose real name was Hugo Bleicher, asserted that the agents were found in bed together at the time of their arrest, others who were present, including the Cottets, all recount the same sequence of events as Odette. The following is an account of Odette's arrest in her own words:

About 11pm I was just taking my clothes off when Madame Cottet came up and into the room (that struck me as rather peculiar even though we were very friendly with them) and told me that Louis Le Belge was asking for me. As no-one knew that Raoul was back yet I told him to stay in the room. I went down into the hall and met Henri and some Italians, and a tall thin German from the Gestapo. He had a lot of fair hair, civilian clothes, big blue eyes, very nervy and about 32 years old. There was also a short man with a hat pulled down and a scarf, I could not see his face, and I did not see him again – it might possibly have been Louis le Belge. Henri offered his hand to me but I did not take it. He said, 'I think a lot of you' but I replied that I did not care what he thought. He told me that I nearly fooled him. He said that this was not my fault because my people were bad, (meaning that the French people had talked and been careless). He said he knew Raoul was here and asked me to show him the way; I did not for a minute and a gun was stuck in my back. I thought quickly that if I screamed Raoul might jump out of the window and the hotel was obviously surrounded and he might be shot, so I took them up and went into the room and just said to Raoul: 'there is the Gestapo' and Henri went and arrested him. I knew Raoul had the messages we collected that afternoon in his jacket pocket but he was not wearing his jacket and it was lying on the bed. I managed to swap the jackets and Raoul saw what I had done so put another sports jacket on. I also managed to slip the wallet in my sleeve. We were taken down and out of the hotel and came to a car driven by a civilian. Henri asked if we wanted to go with the Italians or with him and Raoul said that we would go with the Italians. I thought that the chauffer was probably French and might be friendly to us so I caught my stocking in the back seat of the car and managed to slip the wallet under the back seat, I thought that it might not be found for a few days and would give the others more time to get away. I know that the Gestapo never found the wallet. We were taken to the caserne at Annecy and Raoul and I were put in separate rooms.[3]

It is clear from her testimony that Odette suspected her courier of betraying the whereabouts of her and Raoul, as her SOE interrogation officer recorded:

In her opinion Chaillan caused her and Raoul's arrest by telling Henri that the operation to exfiltrate him was refused and that Paul and Raoul's return was expected very soon. Chaillan knew that she had told London that Raoul's return must not be any later than April 14. Chaillan had been told this but he was not told what the BBC message was, nor the spot to which Raoul was going to return, because of doubts that they had begun to entertain about him because of his determination to get Marsac out at any cost. Odette had a meeting with Roger and Riquet at a patisserie at Annecy on the morning of April 12th. At this rendezvous she told him that the operation to exfiltrate Henri could not take place, but she did not give him the BBC message, or the precise locality chosen for Raoul's return.

Chaillan and Riquet were very angry and abused the organization and the British government, they kept on saying that something must be done and that they would tell Henri that something would be possible.

Chaillan said that he could get Marsac out of Fresnes through the instrumentality of Henri, and could send Marsac back to England. Odette told him that this was foolish and that London's orders were to keep quiet, and to wait for Raoul, and that in any case it was better to lose one man than everything. Odette advised Chaillan not to go to Paris but in spite of this he did go. It was on the afternoon of this day that Arnaud, when he heard that Chaillan had gone to Paris, was so furious that he went to Annecy to try and kill Chaillan. Odette thinks that Chaillan must have told Henri that Raoul was coming back no later than April 14th. Chaillan had complete confidence in Henri. Odette's opinion was that Chaillan was extremely stupid or a traitor, and he was not the kind of man one would regard as stupid.

When Odette received the first reply from London with the instructions that they were to 'act according to their discretion with regard to the German Colonel' she had told Chaillan and Riquet that the operation to exfiltrate Henri might not take place until April 18th, i.e. on the 16th, 17th or 18th. They had done this with the idea that Henri would take no steps to arrest any of them – at any rate not until the 18th of April, so they could be sure of being free until that time. As Odette points out, it is difficult to understand why Henri should suddenly have altered the intention he presumably had to leave them free until the 18th and instead arrested them some days earlier. The only explanation that Odette can offer is Chaillan's telling Henri that the operation could not take place, and that Raoul was expected back very soon. Moreover, Henri clearly knew when they were arrested that Raoul was there. From the day of his return to the time he was arrested Raoul contacted nobody, and nobody knew he had come back, so that unless Henri had been told that he was coming back, he had no reason so suppose that his return was imminent and that he was likely to be at St Jorioz. She hid pocket book in back seat of taxi to avoid giving away details of Captain Morel, Giselle and Gils.[4]

Always one to think on her feet, Odette had discreetly signalled to Raoul that they should keep up the pretence of being married. Clearly others would no doubt dispute this claim, but since they had been living as man and wife for some time, there was also the possibility that a few people would endorse their story. Raoul was actually a distant relative of Winston Churchill and it seemed prudent to claim a closer connection. The name Churchill had a certain resonance with the Gestapo, and by claiming a relationship with the British Prime Minister there was a possibility that their treatment as prisoners might be less severe. More importantly for the Resistance movement overall, they now needed to protect other officers in the field at all costs. Raoul and Odette were initially separated from each other and then handed over to the Italians. Odette's personnel file records:

> The Italian N.C.O. behaved very well towards Odette; at midday, although she did not ask, the N.C.O. brought her a message from Raoul stating that he was still alive. The N.C.O. said that he was very sorry for her and the situation was very difficult for a woman, and he would help her. Also, he said that she did not look very well and he would try and get a doctor. Odette stayed in the barracks five or six days. Although she slept in the first room, there was neither a seat nor water, so she spent the day in the N.C.O's office because he was never there. The friendly Italian soldiers gave Odette news daily of Raoul and Odette sent similar messages to

Raoul. Raoul sent messages as a man would to a woman he loved, and this appealed to the Italians.[5]

After a few days Odette and Raoul were transported from Annecy to Grenoble by lorry, and it was during this time that they were able to communicate and consolidate their story. They were aware that they were probably about to be handed over to the Gestapo. Raoul was reluctant to admit to the name Churchill but Odette was insistent on this point. It was 1943 and the war was going very badly for the Germans; she was convinced that the name Churchill would influence the Gestapo in a positive way and this might result in better treatment. Raoul had already been beaten and had sustained a broken finger and injuries to the side of his face. Odette was hoping to protect him from any further harm. There was, in any respect, a certain safety while they remained with the Italians. During their transportations the Italians fed them with oranges and they sang for the duration of the journey. But Odette and Raoul both knew that this was only the Italian calm before the German storm.

Notes

1 The National Archives: SOE personnel files: Captain Peter Churchill, volume 2, ref: HS9/315.
2 *Ibid.*
3 The National Archives: SOE personnel files: Odette Sansom, ref: HS9/648/4.
4 *Ibid.*
5 *Ibid.*

10

INTERROGATIONS

From the moment of her arrest on the night of 16 April 1943 Odette's main objective was to protect her radio operator Arnaud and the British officer Francis Cammaerts. They were still working as undercover agents and it was crucial for the work of the Resistance and Allied Command that they remained free. Both Odette and Raoul were taken initially to Annecy where they were handed over to the Italians. After a period of seven days they were taken to Grenoble where they remained for another week. Odette was then transported to Turin where she spent one extremely disturbed night in a cell with prostitutes before travelling by train to Nice to spend a further seven days. However, the Italians were uneasy about taking responsibility for such a potentially high-profile prisoner and handed her back to the Germans at Toulon. From here she was taken under armed guard to Fresnes prison in Paris and kept in solitary confinement.

After about three weeks, one night some of the women in the other rooms were heard talking and one of the German soldiers heard them and thought that Odette was one of them. Two men and two S.S. women came into Odette's room and pulled her out of bed. One of the women

smacked Odette's face twice. When she remonstrated with
them they laughed at her. The next morning Odette spoke
to the woman on duty and told her that she would like to
speak to the Captain in charge, and gave her name as Mrs.
Churchill. The woman went to give the message, and ten
minutes after, the Captain came into her room, full of smiles,
obviously impressed by Odette's name. Odette told him that
she was disgusted with her treatment of the night before and
told him about her face being slapped twice. The Captain
was full of apologies and did not want Odette to think ill of
all Germans, and was there anything he could do for her to
make up for it? He said he would send a parcel (which he
did), and also he would go and see Captain Churchill and
tell him that she was alright. He talked to Odette for about
twenty minutes and then went away and gave instructions
to a German woman to look after her. This woman visited
Odette once a week to see if she was alright.[1]

As a political prisoner Odette was denied privileges most of
the time, but the Captain occasionally brought her a book
to read. Against considerable odds Odette was also able to
communicate with a fellow prisoner on the floor below, a
woman named Michelle, through a peculiarly constructed
vertical pipe network. Originally the prison had been built
with vertical gaps between the cell walls in order to provide
a heating system, but these gaps were never used as intended.
It was possible, therefore, to communicate with the prisoner
above and below each cell. There were also sounds of life
from outside the prison walls, the hum of traffic, the laughter
of children playing, old ladies having conversations about
the scarcity of food. But it was the frequent communication
with Michelle that helped to maintain Odette's morale. She

was also uplifted by some words that had been carved on her prison cell wall by a previous inmate.

> *Quand j'etais petite, je gardais les vaches;*
> *maintenant ce sont elles qui me gardent.*
> [When I was young I used to look after the cows
> now it is the cows who guard me.][2]

Odette passed daily messages to her fellow inmate down the wall cavity and there was even an occasion when she passed her some food. For Odette, confined to a damp, smelly and permanently dark cell, Michelle provided a life line, a glimmer of humanity amidst a sea of despair.

> When you are in those circumstances it is good to have someone to talk to. I was not feeling brave all day every day. [Michelle] would talk to me when I returned from Avenue Foch and ask 'are you alright?' She was a communist by the way, a wonderful girl. But you could endanger other people by talking so I had to be careful. Nobody knew for instance, that I had ever been to England. I gave her messages to take to my mother when she left prison but she never got them. I do not know what happened to Michelle after she left. It is a comfort of course to talk to another human being, to know that someone knows you exist. You didn't ask many questions and you didn't want to answer any. You just had to accept that everybody was more or less in the same position.[3]

Avenue Foch was the home of the Gestapo headquarters in Paris during the German occupation of France. The buildings contained several rather ostentatious interrogation rooms and during her time at Fresnes Odette was interrogated on twelve occasions. All of these interrogations involved varying degrees of physical torture. But from the outset Odette chose to adopt an attitude of defiance and contempt towards her captors.

> I found that if you treated them in a certain way, like they were your servants, then they had a certain respect for you. I would think as I looked at them: well you are here but what does it matter? You do not exist. I kept my own identity.[4]

The Gestapo clearly wanted to know the whereabouts of Arnaud and Cammaerts. They wanted to permanently destroy the spy networks that were sabotaging their war effort and feeding information to Allied Command. Odette was the only person who knew for certain the whereabouts of the two British agents, for she alone had relocated them. There had been no time between Raoul's parachute landing and their subsequent arrest for Odette to brief him about events that had taken place in his absence. Raoul was interrogated, but with less intensity than Odette. The latter had convinced the Gestapo that Raoul was the nephew of the British Prime Minister, and that as his wife she alone had enticed him into working for the Resistance movement. After a number of traumatic visits to Avenue Foch it appears that the Gestapo was convinced of this relationship. But it is unlikely that this story alone took the heat off Raoul. From the time of Raoul's return, Odette and he were only together for a short while before their arrest. Henri had probably, and as it transpired correctly, surmised that Odette had not yet updated Raoul about the relocation of Arnaud and Cammaerts.

Whatever suspicions Henri had voiced about Raoul and Odette it was certainly the latter who received the more brutal treatment at the hands of the Gestapo. Odette described how her interrogations at Avenue Foch had given rise to mixed emotions:

> I could have told them what they wanted to know just like that! But I felt that it was a duty to be silent. I had been brought up all my life with a sense of duty. But it's no good – I am not marvellous, not brave or courageous. I just make up my mind about certain things.[5]

The torture of captured SOE agents generally followed a similar pattern. Agents were taken individually to a luxurious dining room that housed a long, polished oak table. Here they would sit nervously awaiting their fate, under the pure white, high ceiling that was decorated with crystal chandeliers. They would be lulled into a false sense of security and given a large, rich meal in order to make them sleepy and more prone to lapses of thought processes. Then they were shown into one of the interrogation rooms and deprived of sleep for a period of up to seventy-two hours while they were continually questioned about their mission details and the whereabouts of colleagues.

Some agents managed to swallow their supply of cyanide pills soon after capture, thus avoiding torture. A few broke down and gave away secrets when subjected to continued torture or when family members were threatened. Others, like Odette, displayed a resilient stubbornness that was unyielding in the face of all the torture methods the Gestapo could throw at them. On one occasion Odette was seared on her naked back with a red-hot iron in an attempt to make her divulge information. She recalled looking up in defiance at the portrait of Adolf Hitler that adorned the walls of the large impersonal room and spitting in his direction.

Since the burning hot iron did not produce the desired results, one of the interrogators nodded in the direction of the torturer and gave him a sinister smile. He was certain that other, more extreme torture methods would be able to break Odette's spirit. The handsome young torturer clicked his heels together and prepared his instruments as if for a surgical operation. He arranged them with clinical precision on the top shelf of a steel and glass trolley. Once he was satisfied that all was in order he calmly and calculatingly approached Odette's naked feet with a set of steel surgical pincers. Fixing the jaws of the instrument around the nail head of her big toe and clamping them shut, he slowly dragged the pincers towards his own body until the nail was detached from the foot. He deposited it into a little steel dish on the floor below. The torturer worked his way through all the toes on her left foot before beginning the same process on her right foot. All Odette's toenails were pulled out in a similar manner, one by one, until a pool of her blood turned into a torrent that spread across the interrogation room floor and flowed under the door. Odette remembers gripping the side of her chair until her knuckles were white, and biting her tongue in an effort to take her mind off the excruciating pain that wracked her body. She remembered being overcome by a tremendous feeling of nausea throughout the ordeal but she was determined to maintain her silence.

I thought that everybody must have a breaking point, but if I could think that I was born to endure this – to survive this, if I can think this way, if I can survive another minute then that is another minute of life. If I can think that way, instead of thinking of what was going to happen in half an hour, then it was not my choice if I was killed. They will kill me physically but that is all. They will have a dead body … useless to them. They will have a body, but they will not have me. They cannot have me because I will not let them have me. Once you accept that it is not your choice an extraordinary thing happens, it's a kind of bargaining, some would say with God. Something comes to you, a feeling of grace, I don't know what it is … but it comes. It is impossible to say that you do it by yourself. After they pulled my toe nails out they were going to start on my finger nails but a guard came in the room and stopped them.

The Germans were clever though. They nearly always found someone of your own nationality to torture you. In my case it was a very good looking French man. While he was torturing me I told him 'you are a sick man, you like doing this, you enjoy this work.' He was condemned to death after the war. But who knows? If it were not for the war he might have grown up as a normal man with a wife and family, and nobody would have known that he was capable of such things. As for revenge, you discover that if you think that way you end up as they are, and what is the point of living like that?[6]

Even under this extreme torture Odette did not give away any information. 'I have nothing to say' became her stock answer to all the Gestapo questions.[7]

When the Gestapo realised that physical torture was not going to produce results they decided to try a softer and more subtle approach for a while.

For six months Henri came to see me every day. He was clever, he used to try and break me down that way. He would say 'I went to a beautiful concert last night and thought of you. He would describe the music. He said 'I am coming to fetch you to take you to Paris; you can have a bath and a good meal.' He told me that he was going to take me out to a concert in Paris. But I told him 'Henri, if you ever do a thing like that I will scream so loudly that everyone will know I have been taken out of my cell by force, I will not go to Paris with you!' He did the same thing for Peter [Raoul] but I was not going to compromise with them.[8]

Henri also arranged a short meeting between Odette and Raoul in the hope of gleaning some insight into the minds of both agents. This insight was not forthcoming. Agents were aware of the mind games that could be played by Nazi interrogators and were careful not to betray feelings. They had been trained to keep their faces expressionless in such circumstances. Odette's personnel file states that:

Raoul told Odette that she looked very pale, but Odette thought that it was best to say nothing and talked of other things. Odette told him that she could quite well go on as she was, but she was bluffing most of the time. They all spoke about general things for about two hours. Odette said that she thought Henri only made this short visit in order to see how things stood between Raoul and her, and what their reaction would be to one another. Odette and Raoul behaved very affectionately to each other so that Henri could see that she would never give in to him.

During an earlier meeting Henri had said 'Of course you do not love Raoul, it cannot be?' Odette told him that he was making a big mistake because it was nothing to do with their arrest. Henri said it was a pity she was taking it like that because he could have done something for her. Odette realised that although he was not saying openly that she should work with him, he was trying to get her to say that she didn't love Raoul, so that he, Henri could then ask her to work with him. When Henri saw that it was no good he changed altogether. Henri then told Odette that Raoul was a very lucky man. He then told her that Madame Marsac had been freed after being in Fresnes for only a week. Odette regarded Henri as an extremely dangerous man who did his level best to gain talks about music, etc., and even brought parcels to make her more comfortable so she needed to be very careful not to be taken in by him. On one occasion Henri said to her: 'You are not the sort of person who would wear dirty clothes like that, do let me have one of your blouses and I will get it washed for you.'[9]

Henri tried to sweet-talk his way into Odette's affections in the hope of gaining information, but all his efforts were in vain. Odette was astute enough to recognise his ploy and viewed it as pathetically misguided.

By October 1943 Odette's health had begun to suffer. A priest who was based at Fresnes prison had done his best to bandage her severely lacerated feet and offer what comfort he could, but the effects of torture and incarceration had taken their toll. While they deliberated over the potential extent of Odette's usefulness as a political prisoner, and whether she was or was not related to the British Prime Minister, the Gestapo decided to move her temporarily into a shared cell. Simone Marie Gabrielle Herail, who was a member of the secret services group Mistral, was her cellmate:

> She [Odette] had long ago accepted her sacrifice for her country, an example of this order is unforgettable.
>
> I knew and lived with Miss Odette Sansom from 15th October 1943 to 11th January 1944 in cell 337 Fresnes prison;

she had been for many months in solitary confinement in that prison and when she came to live with me her health was seriously impaired by this inhuman procedure so dear to the Nazis, her weakness was extreme, she could no longer even eat the small amount of filthy repugnant food which was given to us.[10]

Odette's failure to succumb to torture, brutality, artful persuasion and cruelty, confused and angered Gestapo officials. They had been indoctrinated to believe that women were the weaker sex, particularly those who did not belong to the German master race. Odette's defiant spirit and physical endurance was a source of extreme agitation and a lengthy, somewhat ludicrous tribunal was held to determine her fate. Within the numerous and lavish offices of Avenue Foch, Gestapo officials deliberated for some time before sentencing her to death on two counts. They argued that the first count was for being a French Resistance worker, and the second was for being an English spy. This decision was met with some amusement by Odette, who continued to display an attitude of defiance despite her physical weakness. As she received the damning sentence she commented wryly that they really needed to make up their minds, because after all, she could only die once.

I was known as a grande criminale. When they read out the sentence it took away the drama of the situation. I remember thinking, for which country shall I die? I will never know? It was quite ridiculous. A lot of ridiculous things happened all through my captivity. Ridiculous moments saved me, right up until the end. There is an element of comedy in every tragedy. Comedy helps you survive.[11]

As a *grande criminale* Odette was denied any privileges. Her food was given to her through a small trapdoor, and in amounts smaller than those of other prisoners. She was not allowed to visit the shower block and not allowed to leave her door open. Guards were told that they were not to enter into conversation with her and she was denied the use of books or writing paper. Occasionally the German priest was allowed to visit, but these visits were brief. Odette endured her interrogations and tribulations with decorum and defiance.

In the meantime, Raoul was being confronted with the full extent of their betrayal. On reaching Fresnes prison Henri had wasted no time in showing him the evidence of their SOE activities. Sitting at one of the large oak tables in the swish interrogation room Henri had gleefully produced a number of signed statements and information reports for Raoul's perusal. These had been supplied by the man that Odette had always referred to as 'the ever reliable Marsac'. This information gave away all of Raoul's landing grounds with his map references, both for parachute drops and pickups; particulars of felucca operations, showing how they were carried out; the BBC message which meant to blow up bridges and all the map references of the bridges to be blown; the real names and *noms-de-guerre* of every French and British member of Raoul's and Paul Frager's organisation.[12]

Marsac had clearly told Henri everything he knew, although he later claimed, some years after the war, that he had fallen asleep on a train and Henri had stolen the documents from him. Official records, including the post-war testimony of Henri, confirm otherwise. Furthermore, Marsac's secretary had frequently visited Odette at the Cottet's hotel and it was clear that their whereabouts had been revealed to Henri via a verbal confirmation from Marsac rather than by any incriminating document. Fortunately, he had not been told where Arnaud and Cammaerts were.

Raoul did not seem particularly surprised by this betrayal and understandably, being the commanding officer, he had a clearer perspective in terms of the overall situation than did his female comrade. Raoul's personnel file records his first interrogation:

> Knowing Marsac, I was sure that he had not only given my real name but also exaggerated the relationship between the Prime Minister and myself, which in point of fact I believe is sixty-second cousin. I told Henri that I was distantly related, and his reply was: 'I advise you to say that you are closely related, as it may do you some good.' I should say that during the train journey between Nice and Toulon Lise (Odette) and I spoke through the windows of our two compartments, and decided to maintain the lie that we were Mr. and Mrs. Churchill. We did in fact keep this up, although everyone else of course had said in their evidence that we were not married. I suspected Henri to be a double agent.[13]

Back at SOE headquarters the news of Raoul's arrest was received with considerable frustration and annoyance. Almost a year after the event, a memorandum written by 'F' revealed a highly critical appraisal of Raoul:

> For your personal information he was arrested by the Gestapo the night after his arrival (on his third trip) near Annecy, largely I fear because he neglected the precautionary instruction not to return on any account to any place where he was known from a former visit. Peter is an exceptionally brave, rather reckless young man, who is ideal for leading a smash and grab

party, but has not got the clandestine sense which is so much a weapon in the armoury of our best organizers.[14]

All agents were fallible, however; Raoul was by no means the only agent to make a mistake, and officials working in the safety of London offices had no cause to cast aspersions on those who were fighting for their very survival. In fact, far more mistakes were caused in the field by staff errors in London than by agents working in the occupied territories. Besides which, Henri had been on Raoul's trail for some time. He had also spent some considerable hours thinking about his fate.

At this point in time, the high-ranking Nazi officer Rudolf Hess was being held prisoner by the Allied Command, and it seems that Henri vainly harboured the hope that the British government could be persuaded to exchange Hess for Raoul. Indeed, he proposed this idea to the latter during one of his interrogations. Raoul predictably greeted the suggestion with ridicule. With some conviction, he informed Henri that the British government would never contemplate such an exchange. Since Henri's plan for an exchange was thwarted, on 2 March 1944 Raoul was taken to Sonderlager A in Oranienburg. This was a small camp that lay very near the walls of Sachsenhausen concentration camp.

In the meantime, Odette's interrogations continued until it became crystal clear that no information would be forthcoming. On 12 May 1944 she left Fresnes in handcuffs and under armed guard, and was taken to Karlsruhe where she remained in a prison cell for two months, sharing her accommodation with three German criminals. Then, in July, she was transported with a group of Russian women, in appalling conditions with no food or water, to Frankfurt am Main. On her arrival Odette was imprisoned in a single iron mesh cage. The cage measured five feet long, four feet wide and six feet high. Later in the day, two other women were also thrown into the cage. There was no sanitation, no water and very little food. From Frankfurt she was transported to Halle and placed in a prison loft with forty-five other women. Following an uncomfortable period of five days in Halle, Odette was transferred to the notorious Ravensbrück concentration camp along with six other female agents.

> We did what women do when they are together in difficult circumstances. We tried to keep our spirits up. We exchanged views and talked about people from the London office. Some of them were unsure about certain people in London. When you are captured you look for reasons. They had had time to think. Where was the source? You search endlessly.[15]

Odette and her comrades feared that there was either a traitor in the London office, or that Germans had infiltrated the radio network codes. These fears were not without foundation, and as early as spring 1943 several British agents were being parachuted behind enemy lines straight into the arms of the Gestapo. Even Odette's beloved friend and radio operator Arnaud, who was temporarily saved by her silence, was dropped directly into enemy hands some months later and fatally shot. London SOE officials later claimed that this tragic incident was caused by an 'unhappy staff error'. Unaware of Arnaud's untimely death and the extent of Marsac's betrayal, Odette continued her weary journey with her comrades to Ravensbrück. Tired, hungry but still defiant, on the evening of 18 July 1944 they arrived at the imposing and stench-filled concentration camp. Odette remembered her first impressions vividly:

They were not organized to receive me and I spent my first night on the concrete floor of the shower room. Then I was taken to an underground bunker, a small cell – the window was completely blocked – bricked up. I was in solitary, always in solitary. But you could hear everything and people were screaming. Every evening a procession of women came to be beaten. I could count every stroke. They put me in a cell next to the punishment cell. This was also a punishment in itself of course.[16]

Punishment beatings were recorded as being a necessary discipline for rebellious prisoners and usually involved between twenty-five and fifty strokes to the body, administered by a whip, a stick or a buckled leather belt. In reality, most women were beaten in the punishment block until they fell unconscious or died.

Ravensbrück was a living hell for all inmates. It was a concentration camp built by the Nazis specifically to incarcerate women, but its purpose was to put fear into the hearts and minds of men. For Odette, it was supposed to be the end of the line. Ravensbrück had been chosen by the Gestapo as her place of execution.

Notes

1 The National Archives: SOE personnel files: Odette Sansom, ref: NS9/648/4.
2 Imperial War Museum, oral history interview with Odette Hallowes, 1985.
3 *Ibid.*
4 *Ibid.*
5 *Ibid.*
6 *Ibid.*

7 *Ibid.*
8 *Ibid.*
9 The National Archives: SOE personnel files: Odette Sansom, ref: HS0/648/4.
10 *Ibid.*
11 Imperial War Museum, oral history interview with Odette Hallowes, 1985.
12 The National Archives: SOE personnel files: Captain Peter Churchill, volume 2, HS9/315.
13 *Ibid.*
14 *Ibid.*
15 Imperial War Museum, oral history interview with Odette Hallowes, 1985.
16 *Ibid.*

11

RAVENSBRÜCK

The village of Ravensbrück can be translated in English to 'the bridge of ravens', and it is situated about ninety kilometres north of Berlin. The imposing concentration camp that bore its name was constructed by the Nazis in 1938 and continued to expand throughout the war. Originally the camp was designed to hold 4,000 women prisoners, but by the end of the war this number had increased to around 108,000. The distinctly peculiar and sadistic leader of the SS, Heinrich Himmler, had decided that an all-female concentration camp would serve as a stern warning to all men who resisted German occupation. Moreover, Himmler, who firmly believed that he was the reincarnation of the famous warrior Frederick Barbarossa, took an active role in both the construction and administration of the camp. Therefore, his dubious thought processes permeated its sadistic punishment ethos, labour processes and racial selection procedures. Between 1939 and 1945 it is estimated that approximately 130,000 women were interned at some point in the living hell of Ravensbrück. It is also estimated that about 100,000 of these women died. They were either gassed, shot, buried or burned alive, killed by lethal injection, worked or starved to death, strangled, or killed as result of medical experiments.

The administrators of the camp were a mixture of male and female personnel, but the prisoners were supervised by brutal and sadistic SS women guards known as *Aufseherinnen*. These women were considered to be a breed apart from the normal German house *frau*: cold, cruel and vicious, they took extreme pleasure in devising a variety of torture methods for their hapless victims, and in inflicting the maximum punishment on their wretched bodies. Indeed, punishment beatings only came to a halt when the victim fainted and the SS guards could no longer elicit the desired reaction. Most *Aufseherinnen* began their murderous careers in Ravensbrück, and over 4,000 SS women were systematically trained in sadistic punishment and torture techniques there before moving on to other concentration camps.

Inmates were classified according to their race and were required to wear colour-coded triangular badges for identification purposes. Many of them had their heads forcibly shaved and all were treated with a level of extreme callousness and cruelty that has since been described as inhuman. Polish women outnumbered those from other German-occupied countries, but the ethnic structure of the camp overall varied continually according to the shifting fortunes of war. The captives were usually innocent of any crime apart from that of not conforming to the German ideal of an Aryan super race. If the Gestapo figures are to be believed, then over eighty per cent of the inmates of Ravensbrück were considered to be political prisoners. They consisted of Jews, gypsies, homosexuals, supposedly inferior Slavic races and those who were labelled as 'feeble-minded'. Although designed initially as a camp for women, small satellite sections were later established for male prisoners and a youth camp was built nearby named 'Uckermark'.

The layout of Ravensbrück originally consisted of a series of accommodation blocks, administrative buildings, two shower houses and a bunker. The latter was in effect a jail within a jail and known as the punishment block. There was also a special 'guinea pig' block. As part of a bizarre and futile attempt to create a German super race, SS doctors in all concentration camps conducted experiments on selected inmates. Some of these were prompted by military concerns. High-altitude tests and hypothermic tests were conducted in some camps to ascertain medical information for the German armed forces. For instance, German naval officers wanted to know how long a human being could be expected to survive in freezing cold sea water if their ship was torpedoed. Thus, cold water tanks were constructed specifically to hold live prisoners and the water temperature was simply decreased gradually until the prisoners died. Doctors apparently made their detailed and supposedly scientific notes oblivious to the agonised screams of the dying men.

In Ravensbrück the medical experiments that were conducted on women began in 1941 and focused on gynaecological conditions and sterilisation methods, the testing of sulfonamide drugs on deliberately infected wounds, and the cutting of bone muscle and nerve tissue to test for bone and nerve regeneration. Inmates were deliberately poisoned, had ground glass crushed into purposefully inflicted wounds, were infected with typhus and epidemic jaundice, and were involved with the testing of incendiary bombs. Experiments were also conducted to discern pre-supposed differences in the racial make-up of prisoners. This prompted SS doctors to amass what became known as the 'Jewish skeleton collection'. By the time Odette arrived in 1944 to await her execution, the camp contained prisoners from nearly every occupied territory. A small male camp had also been built adjacent to the original site. Along with their mothers, children of all ages were admitted as prisoners, but most died of starvation. Odette recalled her grim thoughts on walking through the camp for the first time on her way to the bunker:

> I was overwhelmed by the appalling size of the place. The number of women who no longer looked like women, they looked like wounded animals. I was overcome by the sheer misery of it all.[1]

Most prisoners were required to do hard labour, either heavy outdoor work within the compounds, or assisting with the making of parts for the manufacture of V1 flying bombs and V2 rockets. Some also constructed electrical components. There was a roll call in the early hours of the morning after which the women would be given some meagre food and drink before they began their twelve-hour working day. But Odette was classed as an important political prisoner and was exempt from the usual employment. For her, it was simply a silent wait for execution.

By this time, Odette was used to being in solitary confinement. Nevertheless, Ravensbrück represented a dramatic departure from her experience and treatment in Fresnes. In the latter institution, although she had been denied privileges such as books and exercise because she was a political prisoner, she had at least been able to detect signs of normal life. Clandestine communications with another prisoner for instance, unwelcome visits from Henri and the occasional sound of the guards' children cheerfully playing outside the prison walls. In Ravensbrück there were no such diversions. There was just the predictable sound of brutal punishment beatings every evening and the occasional barking and snarling of aggressive guard dogs as they accompanied the SS women on their patrols. Their brutality was legendary. On arrival Odette had been greeted with a fist in her face, simply for bearing the name Churchill. From that date on her treatment varied. Sometimes she was given food and exercise, other times she was starved and beaten. There seemed to be no particular rhyme or reason for these variations in SS conduct. It was clear, however, that the name Churchill held enormous resonance, so much so that Odette was called by the name Schurer for the remainder of her internment. Not surprisingly, this administrative renaming process did nothing to deter the rumours that circulated among SS personnel, and despite the Commandant's efforts to the contrary, Odette became universally known throughout the camp as Frau Churchill. One of the guards, a woman named Truda, was more intrigued than most by the name Churchill and frequently came to talk with Odette:

> She spoke French very well because she had been a governess for many years before the war. I think she was fascinated by the name Churchill. After the war she spent some years in prison. Later, when she was free, she wrote me a letter and said that she would very much like to come and work for me! It was a strange thing but true. It shows you what strange minds some people have, to have been my jailer and then wanting to work for me. But of course the name Churchill was impressive, so impressive that in Ravensbrück they used a different name for me.[2]

While Truda attempted to develop some kind of rapport with Odette, she was an exception. Most of the SS women did not come from educated backgrounds. They were sturdy, physically healthy and tended to gravitate from lower-middle-class families. Some were recruited from the indoctrinated ranks of the League of German Girls, whereas others had responded to general recruitment posters. Technically, the women were not actual members of the SS but Himmler had instructed his male SS officers to treat them as equal in terms of employment and conditions of housing. The women were given Alsatian dogs to assist their work and these were trained to attack inmates at will. Some SS guards took malicious and extreme pleasure in inflicting pain upon their victims, and one even reportedly strolled hand in hand with her boyfriend to watch the punishment beatings every evening. Sadistic, sexual practices were also inflicted on certain prisoners simply for the entertainment of the female guards. Corruption among them was rife and black market drugs and food supplies exchanged hands repeatedly within the prison walls.

Lying in her bunker besieged by loneliness and fear, Odette found it difficult to discern at times whether it was day or night. The SS chief wardress of the bunker block, Margaret Mewes, was supposed to take her out to the exercise yard once a day but frequently forgot, or could not be bothered to take her from her cell. Sometimes the callous but surprisingly attractive brunette guard would also forget to feed her prisoners. As Odette spent her grim and interminably boring days and nights in solitary confinement, she conjured up pictures and events in her mind. She believed that in some extraordinary way, her childhood blindness had prepared her for the ordeal she was now facing.[3]

During her period of blindness, Odette used to replay pictures in her mind and imagine what the world around her looked like. She would think of her toys, her relatives, nature, blue skies, green trees and flowers in bloom. In her underground bunker, with its bricked-up window, she did the same. Day after day pictures and memories of her children laughing, teasing and chattering flowed endlessly through her mind. She pretended that she was back with them, safe and cosseted in the Somerset cottage. By now they would need new clothes and she mentally chose the colours, fabrics and accessories that would complement each of her daughters. When she had visualised each of her daughters in turn, dressed in their new attire, she imagined the changing seasons of Kensington Gardens, along with childhood memories of her coastal walks in Normandy. This ability to use her imagination and construct a level of mental detachment from her prison walls undoubtedly helped to maintain Odette's sanity. But on some bleak and dismal days, even her most cherished and vivid memories were not enough to sustain her will to live, and Odette began to search for sustenance of a different kind.

When I was young I was Catholic. Then I wanted to become a Buddhist. My brother and I read books about it. At eighteen when I married I was nothing. Then one day in Ravensbrück I thought: this suffering by myself is too complicated. I went back to my early Catholic teachings. To this day I can sit at the foot of the Cross and put my arms around God's feet. It is all I have, but that is what I have. It may not exist. I do not even claim that it exists. But I have seen two wonderful things – I call them my miracles. In Ravensbrück I lived for three months and eleven days in the total darkness of an underground cell. One day on my way back to my cell from the hospital I found a leaf that had blown into the compound. There were no trees at Ravensbrück and I cannot tell you the wonder of that happening. Each day they would give us five minutes light in our cells and I would look at my leaf. That was God if you like, but you can't say that to people. You can't say 'That was my God.'

The second miracle was soon after. One day I prayed to God. I was very near to despair. I said to God 'Now I have done all I can – you must take over.' Then the door opened and a plate of food was pushed inside, it was the first plate I had seen for months. Do you know how I felt? I felt very frightened.[4]

At this point in her confinement Odette was covered in scabies and suffering from a glandular condition. Her hair was matted and falling out, and her neck was swollen and painful. The Nazi doctor informed her that she was probably suffering from tuberculosis and offered to operate on her lungs. Odette very wisely refused his offer; the reputation of SS doctors was well known within prison circles. Dr Carl Clauberg, for instance, had killed several hundred women by injecting toxins into the uterus. Those who survived were left with lingering and agonising pain for the rest of their days. But despite her well-founded fears of Nazi medical treatment, Odette's health was undoubtedly deteriorating and on 15 August 1944, as a punishment for the Allied invasion of southern France, the cruel SS guards decided to aggravate her illness.

In total, 94,000 Allied troops had successfully invaded the southern ports of France and had met with little German resistance. The Gestapo correctly assumed that much of the Allied success was due to intelligence information that had been supplied by secret agents such as Odette. Supposedly on orders from Berlin, therefore, the SS guards turned the heating up in Odette's putrid underground cell. This action, coupled with the pre-existing heat of the August weather, almost killed her. For a whole week the heating pelted out at full strength. During this time she was not allowed food and she coped with the heat by dousing her body with cold water from the tap in her room and soaking her sheets in water and wrapping them around her frail body. By the end of the week Odette had developed dysentery, scurvy and a rampant fever. Recalling this time of despair Odette stated:

> I was one minute away from death so often. It would have been so easy to die. It would have been a pleasure.[5]

Not long after this hideous punishment Odette overheard an SS guard informing the camp Commandant that she would not live longer than a week if she were not cared for properly.[6]

With the German armed forces experiencing one humiliating defeat after another, and believing her to be a close relative of the British Prime Minister, the camp Commandant, Fritz Suhren, was not about to lose a potential bargaining tool. Thus, Odette unexpectedly began to receive daily medical treatment in the camp hospital. A course of injections was administered for her scurvy and she was X-rayed and treated with a course of medication for suspected tuberculosis. During these daily treatments a French-speaking nurse at the somewhat austere hospital gave Odette news updates on the state of the war. In a hushed voice as she administered the vitamin injections, she told her of the June landings that had taken place in Normandy. She also informed her of the spontaneous uprising of French Resistance fighters, an uprising that had eventually forced the Germans to relinquish their control of Paris on 25 August.

According to the nurse, a day later General Charles de Gaulle had marched triumphantly towards the Arc de

Triomphe, stopping momentarily to light the flame at the grave of the Unknown Soldier, before continuing to lead his Free French forces down the Champs Élysées. Gleeful crowds cheered his victorious return to Paris, and although a few shots were fired in his direction from an opportunist German soldier, the day belonged to de Gaulle and his supporters. The Germans desperately launched a reprisal bombing raid later that evening in the hope of subduing the jubilant Parisians. The raid was heavy and prolonged, and inflicted substantial damage on central Paris, but it was the last attack of its kind. Within a week all German forces had been ousted from France. The nurse had also heard whispers that on 4 September the Allies had arrived in the port of Antwerp in Belgium. Snippets of news such as these gave Odette renewed hope for the future of Europe. There was no reason for the nurse to lie, of that Odette was certain. With Paris liberated and the Allies rapidly advancing, it was only a matter of time before Germany surrendered.

But as the Allies advanced across Europe, concentration camp inmates bore the brunt of German anger. Food rations were halved, punishment beatings increased and euthanasia programmes stepped up. In Ravensbrück the women continued to suffer and the number of killings increased. In the autumn of 1944 Himmler informed Suhren that he wanted at least 2,000 women to be killed every month. Subsequently, every afternoon certain women were deigned too weak to further the Nazi war effort and were taken to the gas chambers. To avoid panic the women were told that they were being moved to better camps. Some women were gassed in makeshift sheds. They were ushered into the buildings and gas canisters were dropped in from the rooftops. SS guards claimed that it was necessary to leave the engines of their trucks running so that the screaming of the victims could not be heard.

In December 1944 the camp Commandant moved Odette from her underground bunker to an upstairs cell in an attempt to improve her health. Her new cell was a mere six yards away from the camp's number two crematorium. From this point on the terrified cries of the victims and the stench of death never ceased. Women were being burnt alive. With the Allies approaching and Germany on the brink of defeat, Himmler, who had been trying to negotiate a separate peace, paid a visit to the camp to order a further escalation of the killing. A gas chamber had been constructed in close proximity to the crematorium and Odette was witness to the horror of mass extermination.

> The guards had opened a small gap in my cell window to let in some air. The ashes of the dead seeped into my cell every day. My cell was covered with pieces of hair and cinders of the crematorium. I didn't see the victims but I heard them, I heard everything.[7]

Along with the screams of the victims Odette could also hear the repeated chanting of the SS female guards as they beat some of the women to death. Among those who were executed, though unbeknown to her at the time, were her own comrades in arms: Violette Szabo, Lilian Rolfe, Denise Bloch and Cecily Lefort.

> They were such beautiful women. They were all very brave young women. I will never forget them – never.[8]

By the spring of 1945 the Soviet army in the east was advancing rapidly towards Germany, while the British and American forces were approaching from the west. Camp commandants and SS guards alike began to panic in the face of an imminent German defeat. From the beginning of April they had hurriedly implemented a series of ad hoc and ill-prepared plans in a desperate attempt to cover up the gruesome horrors of the Holocaust. Documents were destroyed and lists of prisoners were burned. Incriminating evidence regarding medical experiments was loaded into cars and other vehicles. Extermination programmes that had been accelerated were called to a dramatic halt and over 20,000 prisoners were forced to march from Ravensbrück towards Mecklenburg as the SS made futile attempts to disguise the full extent of their crimes. This feeble and sorry procession became known as the death march. It was clear to all the inhabitants of Ravensbrück that the guards did not wish anyone to be left alive to testify against them. Huddled, frail and feverish in her cell, a resigned Odette prepared to face her execution.

Notes

1 Imperial War Museum, oral history interview with Odette Hallowes, 1985.
2 *Ibid.*
3 *Ibid.*
4 *The London Dispatch*, 30 November 1958.
5 *Ibid.*
6 The National Archives: SOE personnel files: Odette Sansom, ref: HS9/648/4.
7 Imperial War Museum, oral history interview with Odette Hallowes, 1985.
8 *Ibid.*

12

LIBERTY

The days immediately before the Commandant of Ravensbrück finally admitted defeat were tense, tumultuous and dramatic. Commandant Suhren had received orders from Himmler on 16 April 1945 that all prisoners were to be executed forthwith. His instructions insisted that no witnesses should survive to testify to the horrors of the camp. Suhren, however, did not entirely comply with these orders. The reasons for this dereliction of duty are not clear. Many of the male SS guards had seen the writing on the wall by this stage and were running away from the scene of their crimes. Some of the SS women with their vicious whips and snarling dogs had also hightailed through the electric fences into the wide blue yonder. From Odette's bunker the sounds of chaos and confusion could be heard above the normal ordered routine; and from the small crack at her window she watched the scenes with some amazement. She was also beginning to think that the guards had forgotten her very existence.

On 28 April Odette experienced her thirty-third birthday in the familiar darkness of her bunker. This was the day that the Russian army advanced quickly and purposefully towards Ravensbrück. As she sat on her rotting wooden bed in her stinking cell she noticed that the camp was eerily silent. The smoke from the crematorium had subsided and the air in the bunker was no longer filled with cinders and other remnants of charred bodies. She was almost certain that the current state of turmoil was due to an imminent Allied victory but could not understand why the furnaces of the crematorium had suddenly stopped working. She had no idea of the number of prisoners that were being marched forlornly to their death. There had been many occasions during her internment when she had fantasised about liberation, the form it would take, the joy of being released, the sight of the world beyond the electric fences and the wondrous moment when she would see her children again. These thoughts and her renewed religious faith had kept her going while she festered in the obscurity of her bunker. But now, all she could contemplate was her execution. She was a clever woman, and astute enough to realise that the Nazis would not want to leave evidence of their crimes against humanity. As she reflected on her time in Ravensbrück, she considered the SS women who had sadistically taunted, whipped and beaten their victims; she shuddered momentarily and fervently hoped that her execution would be swift.

By now Odette was in an extremely poor state of health; she weighed less than six stone and her emaciated body was covered in lice. Her previously luxuriant thick, black, curly hair was now thin, waist-length and matted, and her skin was ravaged by scurvy and scabies. She was certain that the SS guards were planning to kill her and was resigned to her fate. She had no knowledge of the events that were unfolding outside her cell.

The German military was in complete disarray. Two days after Odette's birthday Hitler had committed suicide by taking a cyanide capsule and shooting himself in the head. The Commandant of Ravensbrück was reportedly devastated. Indeed, he had broken down and cried like a baby when he heard the news. On 1 May an SS guard violently kicked down the door of Odette's bunker and demanded that she pack her things and follow him into the compound. Blinded temporarily by the sunlight, Odette stumbled haltingly outside and stood on the concrete floor of the exercise yard. As her eyes adjusted to the light she put her hands above her eyebrows and looked hesitantly around at the pandemonium. She was confronted by the most hideous of sights, scenes of carnage that sickened her and haunted her mind forever:

> I saw the most dreadful things that other human beings can do to other human beings. I think that animals do it to each other probably, in certain circumstances. It is a very sad spectacle.
>
> Not that I wish to remember … but I can never forget it so … One example I can give you:
>
> I was left in the camp for a moment. I saw a girl about eighteen or nineteen. She had not been there long because she was still fresh. Her head was shaved but she was still fresh looking. The next minute she was dead at my feet. They shot her down and the women around her attacked her, like dogs, she was still warm. But you know they were starving, they were demented, they were crazy. This situation can exist today, if you have a plane crash in the middle of nowhere. People have to survive, and they survive by any way they can find.[1]

Odette was still reeling from the horror of the young girl's death, and the subsequent cannibalistic attack on her body, when she was grabbed aggressively by an SS guard and ushered into a white Mercedes-Benz. Commandant Suhren sat impatiently in the driving seat alongside his deputy. A physically strong, authoritarian man, he was not about to sacrifice his life for a dead leader and the disintegrating Nazi Party. Earlier that day he had built a bonfire, and had tried to burn all the records and names of the women who had died. But there were too many records and not enough time to destroy them. He needed to escape the wrath of the Russians. Therefore, SS guards had frantically loaded boxes of medical and administrative records into the boot of the Mercedes. As he explained to Odette, the Russians were advancing far too quickly for him to casually attend to a bonfire. In an attempt to avoid Russian retribution for his war crimes, he had decided to implement a plan of his own and appeal to American mercy. As Odette indignantly recalled, Suhren knew that he would not survive at the hands of the Russians so was obviously hoping to gain some favour with the Americans and the British. He even plied Odette with good red wine and a picnic en route to the American lines:

> It was ridiculous that with all his authority and dedication to Hitler and all that, a man who could see over a hundred thousand women die without batting one eyelid should choose to take me from my cell and save me.
>
> We were travelling all day and all night. He said 'Do you want to know where we are going?' I said 'No'. I honestly believed that like many other people he would take me to some wood and therefore there would be no traces of me, but he said, 'Well I'm taking you to the Americans.' I said, 'You are? You must be mad!'

But it was true, at about ten o'clock we were stopped by the Americans, he said 'this is Frau Churchill she has been my prisoner.' And I said 'this is the commandant of Ravensbrück you make him your prisoner!!' They took his gun, broke it and gave it to me and I was left in this wonderful white Mercedes lined with white leather and they said, 'we are going to find you a room for the night.' I said, 'If you don't mind, I have not seen the stars for a very long time, I would like to sit in this car until morning.' I had two reasons for doing this, one, I really did want to see the stars, but two, I knew that there were a lot of documents in the car and I wanted to look at those documents and bring them back to this country [England], and I did, I brought them back here. The chief of Ravensbrück thought that I was someone of importance, someone who could help him to a better future. I don't know what he expected.[2]

Certainly a hastily prepared picnic accompanied by a bottle of red wine was not going to save Suhren. His fate was now sealed.

A fresh-faced young American soldier covered Odette with a blanket while she sat in the passenger seat of the beautiful car and gazed at the stars with a strong sense of wonderment. Throughout her first night of freedom she reflected on her time in captivity and her unexpected liberation. There was not a single doubt in her mind that it was the name of Churchill that had saved her life.

There is no other reason why I should have survived, because I was condemned to death, and after all, I am the only one of all the girls who did the same job who was condemned to death who came back. So how else can I explain this? Furthermore, [the Nazis] had every right, if you like, to carry out the sentence. They should have done it. They were the masters of the situation.

Prime Minister Winston Churchill was wonderful. He kept up the story that Peter Churchill was closely related to him. He never said for one minute 'it isn't true.' I thanked him after the war. He said 'Madam, this is indeed an honour.' It was lucky.[3]

It is likely that the Prime Minister perceived some of his own stubborn character in the personality of Odette. He had told French leaders on the eve of their capitulation that Britain would 'fight on for ever and ever'. That same summer, when Lord Halifax asked if he would consider transferring the government to Canada, Churchill disarmingly replied that if the Germans invaded, 'I shall take a rifle (I'm not a bad shot with a rifle) and put myself in the pillbox at the end of Downing Street and shoot till I have no more ammunition.'[4]

By now, however, an Allied victory was assured and, as many historians have noted, an Allied victory in France put paid to any prospect that Germany could avoid defeat. 'The war was won,' Eisenhower concluded in his final report as supreme commander, before the Rhine was crossed.[5]

The French Resistance and the SOE had played an important role during the war and the successful Allied invasions of France had relied heavily on the information supplied by these organisations.

Odette had also completed her own unique role and returned to England on 8 May where the people of Britain were celebrating the long-awaited Victory in Europe. Street parties were in full flow, family reunions were taking place across the length and breadth of the country, and despite the bombed-out cities and the continued imposition of rationing, the British people were imbued with a mixture of joy, relief and optimism. Union Jack flags adorned the streets and buildings, sturdy tables were positioned outside every home laden with food, and music could be heard in every neighbourhood. British naval vessels of every size and shape signalled a siren of salute along the coastline. To some extent, this welcome return to her adopted homeland after the confines of Ravensbrück seemed slightly surreal. Odette laughingly claimed that she only realised she was back in England when she visited a dentist soon after her arrival:

> I had developed an abscess and I was put in a taxi and sent to Harley Street. There an impeccable gentleman greeted me. 'Sit down,' he said. 'Open your mouth.' He examined me as though I looked perfectly ordinary. Then he said quietly: 'I understand you were a prisoner of the Germans.' I said 'Yes.'
>
> 'Ah' he said, 'how very tiresome for a woman.' Then I knew that I was back in England – the land of the stiff upper lip. But nothing has ever done me so much good. The war didn't matter any more. To this day I love that dentist for it.[6]

The abscess was actually the least of Odette's problems. The lack of light during her months of internment had taken its toll on the condition of her skin, hair and bones. One of her toes had also developed sepsis. Several doctors were consulted about the seriousness of her condition, and according to her family and friends her life was saved by the promptness and dedication of Dr Markowicz, a medical officer who replaced her original doctor. He also provided SOE officials with evidence of her suffering:

Euston 2634

Dr Adler cared for Odette from June 1945 onwards and confirmed that:

Odette was in a state of high nervous tension, the nails on her toes were missing and there was a rounded scar on her back.

She was treated with numerous injections of calcium, artificial sunlight and intense medicinal treatment.

T.Markowicz M.D. (sgd)[7]

Odette stated that she had learnt to walk on her heels in prison because of her lack of toenails, and for the first two years after the war she was forced to wear men's shoes while her toenails struggled to grow back to normal.

I have had many operations since the war. Several times they have come to say goodbye because I was expected to die. But I have lived, and I have never had nightmares. Do you know why? Because I think that I have seen such terrible things … such dreadful things. And yet such beautiful things. And it doesn't matter any longer what anyone does to me. I will always recover. I shall always get better but I shall lose something each time. Everything leaves a scar. You see, I am waiting for death. It will be a good friend when it comes, and it will be very sweet. A lot of me belongs to it already. I am already very dead.

Ravensbrück destroyed something inside me, people do not understand.[8]

In addition to her physical weakness and assorted ailments, Odette was spiritually and emotionally weary. This weariness only subsided when she was reunited with her children. But she desperately needed rest and recuperation.

At this point she also decided that her marriage to Roy Sansom was over and reverted to her maiden name. Her commanding officer Captain Peter Churchill had also survived the war and had demanded an early demobilisation in order to care for Odette. He had spent his internment in Sonderlager A in Oranienburg. His prison cell was in a small camp situated near the main walls of Sachsenhausen concentration camp. An official letter from an SOE secretary, dated 24 August 1945, confirms that Peter and Odette were living together in a cottage belonging to a Mrs Lippold in Culmstock soon after the war.

Dear Peter,

I am sending you separately a month's supply of sweet and cigarette rations for Odette and a fortnight's ration for yourself. I am afraid they would not give me your last fortnight's ration as apparently you are officially out-posted. Odette's ration has been debited against her account but as your account has been closed could you let me have four shillings and sixpence the next time you come to the office? Vera is on leave at the moment but before she went she made enquiries about Mme. Brailly's visa to come to this country and the department concerned has told me that there was a slight hitch but that it has now been cleared up and everything is now going to plan. I do hope that you are both enjoying your rest and that Odette is feeling much better.[9]

Vera Atkins, the official administrator for the SOE French Section was trying her best to track down and discover the fate of Odette's comrades. In the meantime, Odette was attempting to pick up the threads of her life and re-establish her loving relationships with her children. In fact, all Odette really desired was to be left alone to live in peace with those she loved. She had suffered extreme physical, mental and emotional torture and merely wanted to move forwards and live a normal life as a housewife and mother. When a newspaper reporter asked her about her plans for the future, she had replied with some conviction:

I am going to stay home and do some knitting![10]

The British War Office, however, had other plans for Odette. As Captain Churchill's letter to Vera Atkins on 29 September 1945 records:

Major Tickell of the War Office Public Relations Department is most anxious to get our story.[11]

Whereas Odette had calmly visualised a post-war future that would be dominated by the needs of her children, the War Office visualised her future as a national heroine. Odette would provide good publicity for the hitherto unheard-of SOE.

Precisely how Odette was persuaded to enter this media circus is not entirely clear. She was a humble, quiet, charming and unassuming woman. Certainly Captain Peter Churchill was fond of publicity and was very persuasive. But it is probable that War Office officials heavily influenced Odette by stating that she had a duty to tell her story. It was now known that her comrades had most likely perished. Therefore, officials argued, Odette was the only person who was in a position to explain the extent and nature of their work and their suffering; and the only way she could possibly accomplish this duty was by recounting her own experience. Since *duty* was a key and emotionally loaded word in Odette's vocabulary she felt that she had no choice but to comply with the wishes of the War Office.

Before she could embark on this dubious media voyage, Odette had another duty to perform. Her persecutors in Ravensbrück were about to be brought to account and she was required to be a key witness at the War Crimes Tribunals. This was an important duty that she needed to perform, not only for her comrades, but for all of those who had perished at the camp. Much as she desperately wanted to close the door on her past and sit quietly by the fireside with her knitting, she also needed to confront the wickedness of her SS tormentors. In the name of justice, therefore, Odette was required to mentally relive the horrors of Ravensbrück and recount them for all to hear in the British military court in Hamburg.

Notes

1 Imperial War Museum, oral history interview with Odette Hallowes, 1985.
2 *Ibid.*
3 *Ibid.*
4 Overy, R., *Why the Allies Won* (London, 1995), pp. 265–266.
5 *Ibid.*, p. 179.
6 *The London Dispatch*, 30 November 1958.
7 The National Archives: SOE personnel files: Odette Sansom, ref: HS9/648/4.
8 *The London Dispatch*, 30 November 1958.
9 The National Archives: SOE personnel files: Captain Peter Churchill, volume 2, ref: HS9/315.
10 *Daily Telegraph*, 21 August 1946, interview with Odette.
11 The National Archives: SOE personnel files: Captain Peter Churchill, volume 2, ref: HS9/315.

13

COUNTING THE COST

Following the German surrender in May 1945, Allied Command established an International Military Tribunal to bring to trial, judge and sentence all Nazis who were suspected of having committed war crimes. As the true horrors of the concentration camps were revealed, people across the world recoiled with an enormous sense of shock and disbelief. One BBC correspondent broke down as he described the scenes on the day that Belsen was liberated, and proclaimed that it was the worst day of his entire life. Piles of corpses were surrounded by the diseased and seemingly soulless bodies of the survivors. It was impossible for the majority of ordinary people to comprehend such a scale of inhumanity. Such scenes were repeated at Ravensbrück, Dachau, Auschwitz and numerous other concentration camps. The cost in human terms was devastating. It was estimated at the time that between 13 and 15 million Jews had been killed in the Holocaust, and the number of gypsies, homosexuals, political prisoners and the so-called 'feeble-minded' and mentally ill also ran into millions. In addition, Nazi doctors and nurses had supervised the euthanasia of children, the systematic killing of the newborn and lethal programmes of medical experiments.

In August 1945 the London Charter outlined four separate categories of war crimes: planning, initiating and implementing wars of aggression; conspiracy to commit crimes against peace; violations of the laws and customs of war; and crimes against humanity. Accusations of war crimes were brought against Nazi leaders, doctors, nurses, scientists and SS concentration camp guards. Those accused were tried by Allied judges and given official counsel by both American and German lawyers. The extremely lengthy, complex and grim tribunals were held in Nuremberg and Hamburg. These cities were chosen because of their symbolic importance to Hitler and his Nazi cronies. They were previously the sites of massive Nazi rallies, Nazi administrative apparatus and Nazi-era architecture. For the German people the location of the courts was designed to be a humbling and humiliating representation of their defeat; and of the ultimate failure of the German master race to conquer Europe.

This symbolism was not lost on the accused, or on the witnesses that testified at the trials. Hitler's commanders were some of the first to be tried, and they attempted not only to efface the stain of their defeat, but also to shift the blame for all their actions onto their late departed leader. As *The Times* reported with some dismay:

> Within the German Officer Corps concerted attempts are being made by surviving military leaders to show that it was Hitler, not they, who was principally to blame for defeat in the field, and that it was the S.S., and not the regular army, which bore the whole guilt for Nazi Germany war crimes. Yet – the latest convictions rest upon a massive weight of evidence, for the German staffs wrote everything down and were caught upon the run. Whatever the verdict in the trial

which is still to come, this evidence must, by its gruesome exactness and detail, for ever destroy the claim that Hitler's commanders had no responsibility.[1]

In the event, the International Military Tribunal that convened in Nuremberg in October 1946 sentenced twelve commanders to death by hanging, including Hess, Göring and von Ribbentrop. Seven others, including Albert Speer, were given variable prison sentences. The medical tribunal convened for the first time on 25 October and several doctors and nurses were also sentenced to death by hanging. In total, there were three Ravensbrück tribunals. Trials for SS guards and some doctors and nurses were held in Hamburg, and it was here that Odette was called to give evidence.

On the morning of 16 December 1946 Odette, her feet protected by cotton wool bandages and oversized men's black shoes, walked confidently into the Hamburg war crimes courtroom and surveyed the scene. Clad in her official First Aid Nursing Yeomanry uniform she looked up towards the gallery where she could clearly see her former persecutors. Alongside their male partners in crime, and perched on high-backed wooden chairs, seven female SS guards sat in silence as they awaited the outcome of their trial. Nearly all of them were attractive, and they would not have looked out of place in any normal crowd of women. There was no obvious clue to indicate their sadistic nature. Yet these were the women who had supervised dreadful atrocities, who had taken such immense pleasure in inflicting pain and suffering. With the crack of a whip and the snarling of dogs they had ushered women and children into the gas chambers and the crematoria. Looking at their cold and almost serene faces, Odette was momentarily taken back in her mind to the harsh obscurity of the Ravensbrück bunker. The ridiculous 'Heil Hitler' salutes resounded in her head. The absurd clicking of heels, abrupt commands, the desolate faces of prisoners in the exercise yard who had long since given up the will to live, the girl who was shot dead at her feet – all these memories and more flooded back as she walked calmly up to the witness stand and swore her oath. The newspapers duly reported her testimony the following day:

> Mrs Sansom said that she saw screaming and struggling women dragged to the crematorium. Doors opened, the women disappeared, and then the doors closed again. She heard more screams and then there was silence. The women did not come out again. Mr C. L. Stirling, the Judge Advocate General, saying that the witness had made a most serious accusation, asked whether she swore that the women were burnt alive. She replied that all she could swear to was that she saw them taken to the crematorium.[2]

For Odette and other key witnesses the process of giving evidence was a traumatic one. Indeed, the trial transcripts make for very uneasy reading. Within the overall court proceedings one of the most shocking revelations was the prominent role that had been played by members of the medical profession. Another witness, a Dutch woman, who had also spent time in the notorious Ravensbrück bunker, gave a particularly moving account of her experiences in the camp hospital:

> She said that all the prisoners feared to go into the camp hospital because, with very few exceptions, none came out alive. One of the accused, a man named Binder was satisfied, said the witness, only when he saw blood. She was sent to

the bunker where she spent six weeks. The building was artificially made cold, and although it was summer her feet swelled and her hands became numb. One day Dorothea Binz, a wardress, came to the door and shouted, 'here you will starve,' and beat her into unconsciousness.

Vera Salvequart used to give to patients a white powder, and, if that did not work, an injection, 'to help them into a better world.' The witness had seen Salvequart knock gold teeth out of the mouths of the dead. In the jugendlager, where the gas chamber was installed, there was a death roll, on average, of twenty-five prisoners a day, besides those who perished in the chamber itself. Among the punishments imposed was deprivation of the midday or evening meal every day from one week to four weeks. One woman was made to stand up from morning until evening. Beatings ranged from twenty-five strokes, to fifty or even seventy-five. The witness, a midwife, was arrested in The Hague in 1941 for advising a couple to name their child after Queen Wilhelmina.[3]

The men and women accused gave various excuses for their criminal actions. These supposed justifications ranged from 'I was merely conducting scientific research' to 'I was merely following orders.' All of the accused attempted to portray themselves as humanitarian. This attempt seemed all the more ridiculous considering the vast amount of evidence to the contrary. Some of those accused even claimed to be victims of the system, including the head nurse of Ravensbrück, Elizabeth Marshall. Yet witnesses testified that on one occasion Marshall had given an order for over fifty prisoners and their newborn babies to be loaded into a truck with no food or water; all of them died. She had also stockpiled baby milk that had been supplied by the Red

Cross while simultaneously allowing newborns to die. The prisoners were unable to breastfeed their infants because of their own poor nutrition.

Many of the Nazi war criminals were not brought to trial immediately, however, and some, who had gone on the run, were never brought to account for their crimes. Writing in 1949 with particular regard to the medical crimes that were perpetrated under the Nazi regime, Andrew Ivy, an American physician who had testified for the prosecution, noted:

> What happened to the medical profession in Germany is stern testimony to the fact that acceptance of or even silence before anti-Semitism and the rest of the trappings of racism, acquiescence in or even silence before the violation of sacred professional ethics, the service by medical men of any goal but truth for the good of humanity, can lead to dishonour and crime in which the entire medical profession of a country must in the last analysis be considered an accomplice.[4]

In many respects, the trial of Nazi doctors was a whitewash of professional misconduct that shifted the blame for atrocities away from doctors and onto the apparatus of the German state. While Andrew Ivy apportioned blame to state interference in medicine, officials of the American state seized all Nazi medical research. Furthermore, leading Nazi scientists were given positions of power within pharmaceutical industries, university laboratories, NASA space programmes and military research stations. The beginning of the Cold War had rendered Nazi medical research on humans an invaluable asset to American strategic policy.[5]

The tribunal judges deliberated over the gruesome and unprecedented volume of evidence for several months, and considered numerous defence pleas of mitigation before reaching their final decisions. In respect of the first Ravensbrück camp trial, all sixteen accused were found guilty in the Hamburg war crimes court on 3 February 1947, and eleven death sentences were passed. One of the accused, a Dr Winkelman, died of a stroke before hearing his death sentence. The Hamburg court passed the following sentences:

To die by hanging: Carmen Mory, forty-one-year-old Swiss-born journalist, block leader at the camp, accused by the Germans of spying for the French, and accused by the French of spying for the Germans; Vera Salvequart, nurse who administered lethal injections; Dorothea Binz, head wardress and chief of the punishment block who used to cavort and laugh with her boyfriend as they watched the prisoners being abused; Elizabeth Marshall, aged sixty, matron of the camp 'hospital'; Greta Boesel, head of women's labour gangs; Johann Schwartzhuber, deputy camp commandant; Rosenthal, an SS doctor who permanently maimed women by experimental operations; Gustav Binder, camp tailor, accused of 'orgies of beatings'; Dr Percy Treite, deputy medical chief; Ludwig Ramdohr, political interrogator who flogged prisoners to get 'confessions'; and Dr Gerhard Shidlausky, who said that camp conditions were 'beyond his control'.

SS Captain Peters, leader of the SS guard, and Dr Hellenger, the camp dentist, were sentenced to fifteen years' imprisonment. Margaret Mewes, SS wardress, and Eugenia von Skene were sentenced to ten years' imprisonment.[6]

As for Commandant Fritz Suhren, he was not tried at the Ravensbrück trials because he had managed to escape British custody. Nevertheless, he was later discovered and arrested by German criminal police on 4 April 1949 in Grafenan, where he was working as a farm labourer using a false identity. He was then handed over to the French and executed for war crimes at Rastatt on 12 June 1950.

Surprisingly, Odette bore no malice against her persecutors. Despite her considerable suffering at the hands of the Gestapo and the SS guards she remained philosophical and claimed that she felt no bitterness:

> They were sick, very sick individuals. There is nothing else that can be said about them. People used to say to me when I came back, 'you must have such a terrible idea of human beings, you must be frightened almost.' I used to say 'Why?' Nothing has changed. There were always bad people. I've seen a lot of bad people but because of those evil people I have also seen a lot of good people, normal people.
>
> I consider that it has been an extraordinary experience, I feel as though I am a thousand years old and I love people, I really do. There was nothing to be bitter about. Bitterness is a waste of everything, but you have to remember. You must remember because it is a duty to the people who did the right things; to one's brave comrades; to all the good and brave people. There is no point in being bitter and creating the same feelings of hatred. It is pointless and harmful. I am only sad, extremely sad, and will be for the rest of my days, that my comrades did not come back.[7]

Odette also insisted that she had not done anything that could be considered as particularly brave, but felt that she had simply done her duty.

> People do what they can, I suppose. Until you are in those circumstances, how can you judge? It makes me cross when I hear someone say oh, he was weak because he gave away this

or that. How do you know that? Put yourself in his shoes, would you have been stronger? I claim that it is impossible to know it. I was a free agent in a way. I knew that if they were going to torture me, it was me only, not a member of my family. Not a loved one. You can be stronger that way. It is not like someone saying, 'if you do not talk we are going to do this to your husband or mother or children'. Faced with a decision like that who knows what they would do? It is easy to blame.[8]

But despite Odette's forgiving nature, and her intent to carry on her post-war life as a normal housewife, the invisible scars of Ravensbrück had taken their toll on her relationship with her husband Roy Sansom. He was not told of her capture by SOE officials until 12 July 1944, by which time Odette had been in captivity for over a year. On her return to England she found that it was impossible to pick up the threads of her marriage.

It is not clear whether Odette's decision to end her marriage was taken because of her feelings for Captain Peter Churchill, or because of the prolonged and enforced estrangement from her husband imposed by war. Either way, a quick and discreet divorce was arranged for Odette by a highly respectable lawyer named Hugh Park. Hugh had originally served with the Royal Air Force, but in 1942 he had been seconded to the SOE to debrief agents returning from the field. Indeed, the divorce was so discreet that many people simply assumed that Roy Sansom had died during the war. For the British media, however, Odette's subsequent marriage to her former commanding officer seemed to signal a fairytale ending for the courageous heroine of the Ravensbrück bunker.

Notes

1   *The Times*, 3 November 1948, p. 5.
2   *The Times*, 17 December 1946, p. 3.
3   *The Times*, 11 December 1946, p. 3.
4   *Trials of War Criminals*, volume 1, Washington DC, US Government Printing Office, pp. 61–67.
5   Heinmann, Weideraufbau, in Bower, T., *The Paperclip Conspiracy* (London, 1987), pp. 439–440.
6   *The Times*, 4 February 1947, p. 4.
7   Imperial War Museum, oral history interview with Odette Hallowes, 1985.
8   *Ibid*.

1. Studio portrait of Odette, taken just over a year after her release from Ravensbrück concentration camp, when she received her medal. (*Photograph taken from Odette's SOE personnel file, courtesy of The National Archives Image Library*)

AMIENS. — La Place Gambetta.   ND Phot.

2. This is how Amiens would have looked at the time of Odette's birth. (*Author's collection*)

3. A modern view of Amiens. (*Authors collection*)

4. Fresnes prison, Paris, where Odette was incarcerated soon after her arrest in 1943. (*Author's collection*)

5. Ravensbrück concentration camp where Odette was kept in solitary confinement in an underground bunker. (*Author's collection*)

6. Ravensbrück concentration camp crematorium where thousands of women perished. (*Author's collection*)

7. Allied soldiers liberate Paris. (*Courtesy of Franklin D. Roosevelt Presidential Library and Museum*)

8. Liberation of Paris, August 1944. After the fighting, American soldiers embark on some sightseeing. (*Courtesy of Franklin D. Roosevelt Presidential Library and Museum*)

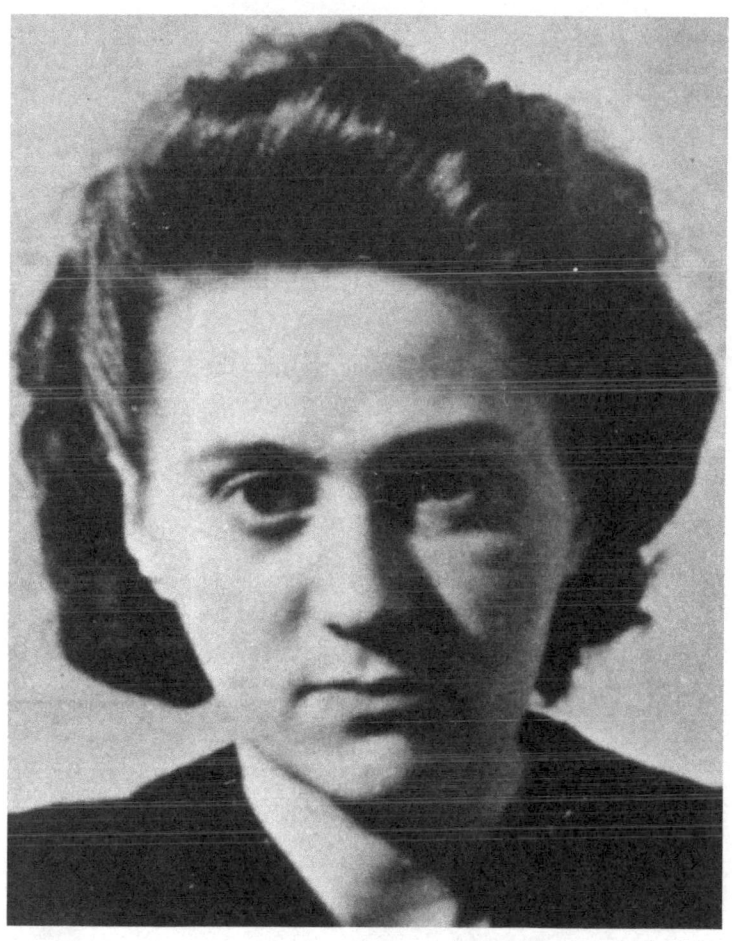
9. Odette soon after her release from Ravensbrück. (*Photograph taken from Odette's SOE personnel file, courtesy of The National Archives Image Library*)

10. A photograph of Odette which has been hanging in 282 ATC
Squadron's headquarters since she became their president in 1969. The
photo is probably of around that date. (*Photograph courtesy of Bob Naeem
Squadron Leader 282 ATC Squadron Royal Air Force*)

11. Odette attending
an annual RAF
Wing Parade
Ceremony as guest
of honour in 1981.
(*Photograph courtesy of
Bob Naeem Squadron
Leader 282 ATC
Squadron Royal Air
Force*)

12. A photograph
of Odette taken at
the new squadron
headquarters
which she was
invited to formally
'open' during 1988.
(*Photograph courtesy of
Bob Naeem Squadron
Leader 282 ATC
Squadron Royal Air
Force*)

13. Memorial plaque to Odette Hallowes rests underneath the general memorial to the members of the Women's Transport Service FANY. The memorial inscription on the plaque dedicated to Odette reads: 'Here she laid violets transforming into service the pain of her survival.' Odette Hallowes was the Vice President of the Women's Transport Service FANY between 1967 and 1995. The plaque is located in the churchyard of St Paul's Church, Knightsbridge, London. (*Author's collection*)

14

DARLING OF THE PRESS

For a woman who merely wanted to relax and do some knitting in the post-war years, Odette may just as well have handed over her knitting needles to someone else entirely. Rather than the calm, serene life she had envisaged, she found that she was caught up in a whirlwind of frenzied activity. Her wartime story that she herself described as being 'more like a bad Hollywood film than a good one' caught the public imagination and she became a celebrated heroine on both sides of the English Channel.[1]

The media, it seemed, could not get enough of her story, and for at least the first decade following her release from Ravensbrück Odette was the darling of the press. There were photocalls, interviews and serialised accounts of her exploits behind enemy lines and subsequent internment at the hands of the Gestapo. Official recognition of her courage was also forthcoming and her personnel file contains a number of recommendations, witness statements and citations, all of which confirmed her heroic stoicism. Initially, Odette was awarded an MBE, but many government ministers and military officers believed that her extreme courage warranted greater recognition, as the following statement from the Honours Committee suggests:

M.O.I. (S.P.) Honours and Awards 10th July 1946

The citation for Ensign Odette Sansom covers a story of almost unexampled courage, endurance and devotion to duty.

In order to strengthen this recommendation for a George Cross statements have been obtained from a woman eye-witness of some of the facts in the citation, from her commanding officer whose life and liberty she saved and from a doctor who treated her for the injuries inflicted on her by torture.

It is very much hoped that this most gallant lady will receive full recognition for her magnificent behaviour and devoted services.[2]

Lt Colonel FCA Cammaerts DSO was among those who bore witness to Odette's bravery and supported the recommendation:

I certify that on the 17th April 1943 when Ensign Sansom was arrested: the Germans knew of my existence and were anxious to trace me. Ensign Sansom was the only person who knew my whereabouts in France.

The Germans also knew that Ensign Sansom had this information. Thanks to her courage and tenacity I was enabled to continue my work without hindrance. I can also confirm that Sansom also knew the contact address for Captain Rabinovitch.[3]

But Odette was a reluctant heroine, and when she was informed by a newspaper reporter that she was about to receive the George Cross she was somewhat bemused.

I didn't even know that the George Cross existed. I was on holiday in a rented cottage with my children when a reporter knocked on my door early in the morning. He said that I was going to receive the George Cross and I told him that I was only renting the cottage and he had probably got the wrong person. He assured me that I was the person he wanted to talk to, but I didn't know what he was talking about! I said 'the George Cross! What is that? I don't know what it is.' Later that evening my eldest daughter also asked me what it was so that she could tell her friends when she went back to school. I said that we would have to find out more about it. I was just tucking her into bed when she laughed and said, 'the George Cross mummy, is that the best you could do?'[4]

On 20 August 1946 Odette donned her uniform once more and travelled to St James's Palace to receive her medal. She was the first woman to receive such an honour. But in her acceptance speech and press interviews, Odette resolutely maintained that she had accepted the honour on behalf of all the women who had served with the SOE, many of whom, she claimed, had done far more and been far braver than she. Moreover, she continued to highlight the work of her fallen comrades in all her subsequent public relations and charity work.

Major Jerrard Tickell, of the War Office public relations department, conducted lengthy interviews with Odette and her former commanding officer Peter Churchill, and wrote a fictionalised account of their exploits in a book entitled *Odette: The Story of a British Spy*. It seems that although Odette was reluctant to be catapulted into the limelight, she was persuaded by the War Office, and Tickell in particular, that this was the only way that she could possibly highlight the work of her SOE friends. The book was published in 1949 and sold over 500,000 copies. Two years before the publication of her story, and to the obvious delight of the British press, Odette had married Peter Churchill. The wedding ceremony took place at Kensington Registry Office on 15 February 1947. As far as the general public was concerned, Odette's story had all the ingredients of a magical fairytale. It was a tale of triumph over disaster, of human endurance in the fight against evil, but most of all, of passionate love that had survived against the odds. Odette became everyone's darling spy. Not that Odette perceived herself in this way – far from it. As far as she was concerned she was merely doing her duty by her comrades.

> When I came back it was always the same thing; I tried to interest people in their story and they would say, 'yes that's very interesting but what did you do?' It was always coming back to me, so I decided that the best thing I could do was to try and give them some publicity, which was started by Tickell's book and then the film. Then I helped with the book about Violette Szabo and I was technical adviser to the film about her life. It started the ball rolling about their stories and that is the only satisfaction I got out of all that.[5]

The decision to make a film adaptation of Odette's story was taken by the producer Herbert Wilcox. American producers also wanted to make the film but Odette held out against an American production. Tickell, who would have made considerably more money by selling his book copyright to the Americans, bowed to Odette's wishes.

The War Office provided special facilities and guidance during the making of the film, and Odette and Peter Churchill acted as advisers alongside Tickell. Wilcox had originally wanted a French actress to play the role of Odette but the latter was insistent that nationality was irrelevant. SOE women had been a range of nationalities and it was their work against the Nazis that she believed should be emphasised rather than their national identity. Eventually, Dame Anna Neagle was chosen to play the role of Odette and the two spent a whole year together in France and Germany before filming began. Anna visited the concentration camps and spent time in the airless bunker of Ravensbrück. She met and spoke at length to numerous French Resistance workers and visited the sites of clandestine meetings, safe houses and parachute landings. According to Odette the actress was visibly moved by her research for the role, so much so that it took her well over a year to recover and feel normal again once filming had finished.

I told him [Herbert Wilcox] that the actress did not need to be French, not all the girls were French and I was just one of the girls. It was not me that I wanted to see up there on the screen, it was the girls. I found in Dame Anna Neagle someone of great honesty and sincerity. They were the two main qualities. Anna was very good in the film, because she had this great simplicity and honesty and she did it with all her heart really. It affected her deeply. I shall always be grateful to her because the film passed the test in places where I thought it would be difficult. It passed the test in Paris. We had a wonderful reception for it. I was a bit worried because I thought now we are in the country where they know it all. It was shown for charity and the critics were positive and said it was the truth and everything. We took it to Belgium where it was also very well received, and in Holland.

I think that people felt the simplicity of it. It really, if you like, wasn't clever. When I think of what the Americans would have done with it. Wilcox toned it down and made it simple even though he had all the material to make it into a Hollywood story.

I am sure that it is difficult for some people to believe some parts of the story, but it did happen the way that it did and I cannot alter the facts. I did survive and I should not have done. I do not take any pride in that because it was nothing whatsoever to do with me. I was lucky if one wants to call it that.[6]

There were, however, several ex-French Resistance members who felt that their contribution was not given due recognition in the film that was entitled simply *Odette*. But the reviews that followed the first showing at the Plaza Cinema, London, on 6 June 1950 were generally positive. *The Times* reported the following day:

She [Odette] is one of the greatest heroines of the Resistance movement, who was caught and tortured, but did not betray. The film, throughout the two hours it takes to run, is almost self-conscious in its conscientiousness, and what faults it has spring from its apparent conviction that a matter of history does not need any imaginative treatment in its presentation.

If then, the picture of the way the Resistance movement went about its work in France does not always carry conviction, correct though in detail it doubtless is, the portrait of Odette as Miss Neagle draws it, is entirely satisfactory. Odette may well stand as a symbol for all the women who suffered in the war, but this Odette is, over and above her symbolic and heroic being, an individual. Miss Neagle shows her as a woman of sense and character, the type that can be trusted with responsibility, and Miss Neagle neither sentimentalizes on the one hand nor dramatizes on the other. Odette is a woman who is removed from the ordinary in courage, but even while she is reiterating her magnificent 'I have nothing to say' in the face of the worst the Gestapo can do, the link with common humanity is never broken.[7]

In many respects, as the critics observed, the film had followed the stark authenticity of Odette's story without undue embellishment. But it was also possible to detect the public relations hand of the War Office and the French Section of the SOE, both in the making and the promotion of the film. Buckmaster and his indomitable and inscrutable administrator Vera Atkins had initiated a well-orchestrated publicity campaign during the immediate post-war years that most of the surviving SOE agents complied with. The film was distributed by the British Lion Film Corporation and all the advisors, other than Odette, were British. The script was written by Tickell, who ensured that the screenplay was based around his book. Buckmaster, Atkins and other members of the SOE also shaped the course of the film. In many instances, therefore, the British agents were portrayed as efficient and heroic while the French were portrayed as incompetent fools. There was also a greater emphasis on the German army as a whole rather than on the Gestapo. This emphasis clearly reflected the concern of the War Office and other British officials with regard to bringing Nazi war criminals to justice, and their fear that German commanders were trying to fudge their part in the atrocities. Tickell was eventually accused by journalists, historians and some government ministers of being economical with the truth.

Odette appeared not to notice the subtle nuances of the film's content. Aside from her own input in terms of personal experiences of torture and imprisonment, it is clear that the film was heavily influenced by Peter Churchill, the head of French Section SOE, Buckmaster and the War Office public relations guru Tickell. Indeed, it can be argued that Odette had more influence as technical adviser over the film of Violette Szabo's life than she did over the way her own story was portrayed. Entitled *Carve Her Name With Pride*, and released in 1958, the Szabo film contained many of the events that Odette later recalled in official interviews about her own life, and it drew distinct parallels with Odette's experience of undercover work, capture and torture. This was not surprising, since both women had undergone the same training principles, but it was as though Odette had finally been given a degree of freedom to portray events as they really were. In contrast, *Odette* had largely conformed to a stifled War Office version of history that not only downplayed the role of the French Resistance circuits, but in places also portrayed Odette as being a mere appendage to her commanding officer. There was an official War Office agenda and gender bias that Odette, in her eagerness to do her duty by her comrades, had overlooked.

Thus, critics observed that Violette's story emphasised the strength, courage and conviction of female agents working in the field far more convincingly than that of *Odette*. It quite rightly emphasised the role of the Gestapo in the capture and torture of female agents rather than shifting responsibility for such matters onto the German army for tribunal purposes. The film was also heavily sanitised in the sense that it did not show the true extent of Violette's torture or the grim reality and length of her internment. For dramatic purposes Violette was portrayed, along with her comrades Lillian Rolfe and Denise Bloch, as being machine-gunned to death by a firing squad, when in reality they were all killed by one SS officer with single shots to the back of the neck. The executions were supervised by Ravensbrück Commandant Fritz Suhren in the presence of a camp doctor and the camp dentist Dr Hellinger. The latter was always present at executions in order to examine the mouths of the dead for gold fillings. If present, these fillings were extracted and the gold used for the German war effort. Gruesome and unpalatable details such as these were not given media attention, and at a time when women were still viewed as a somewhat protected species in British society, it was not considered appropriate to dwell on their experiences of torture. Cinematic representations of SOE women were, therefore, obviously flawed; although they did at least ensure that their sacrifices were acknowledged.

Odette was now clearly branching out, establishing her own professional voice and using her name to highlight charitable causes, such as the Poliomyelitis Trust, that were dear to her heart. Her personal life had also moved in a completely new direction. By the time the film *Carve Her Name With Pride* was released Odette was divorced from Peter Churchill and remarried to another former SOE officer, Geoffrey Hallowes. The causes of her second marriage breakdown were not documented, and as always Odette did not speak about such highly personal matters. But it is likely that the darling of the press had also become very weary of the press. Odette wanted a lower profile whereas Peter Churchill appeared to enjoy the attention. He was a flamboyant character who encouraged newspaper coverage of his activities, and went around the country giving lectures about his wartime exploits. He wrote books about his experiences and worked the public relations circuit for all it was worth. This attention-seeking was anathema to Odette's character.

Yet another serialisation of Peter's story was published in the national newspapers in 1953 and the photographs that were taken in France for illustration purposes revealed the degree of tension and strain between the couple. One picture, of the couple in the small pavement café in Arles where they used to wait for radio messages from Arnaud, shows Odette looking disinterested and bored as she sits opposite her husband at a small table, cigarette in his hand, presumably listening to him pontificating about the war. In another picture Peter and Odette are photographed outside their wartime headquarters in Cannes, Odette is pictured standing apart from her husband, with one hand on her hip, impatiently waiting for the photocall to finish. The couple's happy ending had dissolved around them.

By 1955 Peter Churchill was living a solitary life in the south of France, and it seems that he too had become tired of the press attention. He had also initiated divorce proceedings against Odette on the grounds of adultery with Geoffrey Hallowes. It is highly probable that Odette had tired of her second husband's continual preoccupation with the war. It is also likely that the pressure of being constantly in the limelight for ten years had taken its toll on their relationship. Following her second divorce Odette married Geoffrey Hallowes in 1956.

Geoffrey Hallowes was an entirely different character to Peter Churchill. He was a quietly confident man with a colourful and distinguished SOE career. Odette was six years older than he but this age gap did not affect their relationship. He was also exceedingly rich, since Geoffrey's father was Edward Hallowes, of the eminent Dry Monopole champagne and wine importers Twiss, Browning and Hallowes of London. Geoffrey had returned to work for the family business following his demobilisation and eventually established and became the first director of International Distillers and Vinters. The couple had much in common; they were both by nature very private people and they shared a love of fine wines (Odette was particularly fond of Bordeux).

Geoffrey had also worked in Odette's beloved France with the Resistance. Reputedly, he fell in love with the celebrated heroine following a chance meeting at a charity fund-raising event. For Odette, their relationship was something of a revelation. Her first husband had been much older than she and rather authoritarian, her second husband had been her commanding officer, again authoritarian and always in control. This time her love interest was younger than she and exerted no authority over her. Their love was based on mutual respect, humour, intelligence and shared interests. In the years to follow, Geoffrey Hallowes became Odette's rock and ardent protector. She described him as being 'a truly marvellous husband'.[8]

Notes

1   Imperial War Museum, oral history interview with Odette Hallowes, 1985.

2   The National Archives: SOE personnel files: Odette Sansom, ref: HS9/648/4.

3   *Ibid.*

4   Imperial War Museum, oral history interview with Odette Hallowes, 1985.

5   *Ibid.* Also note that the film about Violette Szabo's story that Odette was referring to is the film *Carve Her Name With Pride*, which was released in 1958 starring Virginia McKenna in the title role.

6   *Ibid.*

7   *The Times*, 7 June 1950, p. 9.

8   Imperial War Museum, oral history interview with Odette Hallowes, 1985.

15

SOE UNDERMINED

At a time when Odette had finally found some emotional security and shelter from the limelight, she was thrust into the public eye once more. This new wave of publicity was prompted by a series of controversial articles and books that were published from the mid-1950s onwards, and questioned the effectiveness and integrity of all SOE officers.

One such book, written by Jean Overton-Fuller, accused the SOE of deliberately dropping agents into the hands of the Gestapo as part of a 'double bluff' scenario. Another, entitled *Death be not Proud*, by Elizabeth Nicholas and published in 1958, suggested that SOE officials in London had known conclusively that the radio networks and codes of certain agents had been infiltrated by German intelligence officers, and that London had been busily relaying false information via these compromised radio networks to deceive the German High Command. Furthermore, Nicholas argued that at least forty-seven agents, French and English alike, had been deliberately dropped into enemy hands to perpetuate this stream of false information. Not surprisingly, the seriousness of these accusations caused a high level of anxiety and disquiet in political circles, and a motion was tabled in the House of Commons by the Conservative

MP for Tynemouth, Dame Irene Ward, who called for a full inquiry into the activities and administration of the SOE.

The research findings of Overton-Fuller and Nicholas merely confirmed the suspicions that were harboured and discussed by Odette and her comrades on their way to Ravensbrück. Their shared experiences had convinced them that at least one person high up in the London SOE administration was a double agent. Odette was entirely sure that this was the case. Moreover, unbeknown to the international heroine, and to Dame Irene Ward, certain sections of her SOE personnel file had mysteriously disappeared. These sections included a substantial part of her debriefing interrogation, where she described her toenail torture, and a signed affidavit that accused a number of people she suspected of being double agents. Those accused included high-up officials within the SOE London office.¹ A number of other SOE files were inexplicably destroyed in an office fire and conspiracy theories began to emerge on both sides of the Channel. By this stage, the French Section of the SOE was receiving a good deal of negative publicity and the War Office public relations team were having enormous difficulty in containing what Buckmaster referred to as 'monstrous' allegations.²

These allegations fell roughly into four categories, the first of which accused the organisation of employing a Nazi spy as one of their operatives during the war. The second accused the SOE of endangering the lives of agents by dropping them deliberately into the hands of the Gestapo, since it was known that certain radio codes had been infiltrated. Thirdly, it was alleged that the SOE did not inform the families of agents who were captured or executed of their fate until long after the event and, fourthly, the organisation was blamed for being amateurish when compared to German intelligence networks.

Buckmaster did his very best to refute such allegations and reluctantly explained some of the successes and flaws of French Section through the pages of the national press in the hope of appeasing his critics.

> The penetration by the Germans in the summer of 1943 of the so-called 'Prosper' circuit was a serious setback to our operations. I have never tried to conceal or minimise the importance of this German success. But it represented one success only – admittedly with grave repercussions and gave rise to a large number of arrests.
>
> It did not stop the progress of the French Section towards its objective – the constant harrying of the German forces and the stranglehold on the German economic machine in France. Like all such experiences it taught us lessons which can be learned only in that way. Those lessons were fully learned. Of the four hundred and eighty Service members of the French Section, one hundred and thirty were caught. The casualty rate in a battalion in the field over four years was much higher than one in four, although it would include those who were injured.
>
> In SOE a member, if injured, did not have the same chance as an ordinary soldier of escaping, and the fate of an SOE agent who became a prisoner was usually death. Couple that with the far greater risks taken by SOE agents, and it becomes inevitable that casualties were fairly high. It has been alleged that we showed callousness and secretiveness towards relatives of the people who worked for us and who were killed or captured. I can only say that all relevant facts were communicated as soon as they became known.[3]

The last part of this statement was not entirely true. Agent personnel files clearly reveal that many of their relatives were not told of their capture or death for months, or in some cases years, after the event. In fairness to Buckmaster, many letters to relatives were handwritten and there were therefore no copies on file. In Odette's case her husband was informed of her capture in July 1944, fifteen months after her arrest, yet the details of her arrest are recorded and confirmed in her file, and that of Peter Churchill's, in May 1943. A memorandum (F/C/17/2719) in Churchill's file dated 28 March 1944 again confirms the circumstances of their capture. However, this delay in communication was often in line with the wishes of the agents concerned. Agents did not want to alarm their relatives unnecessarily and usually asked that communication with regard to their circumstances be delayed until all the facts could be verified. Others had asked people such as Vera Atkins to lie to their relatives about the nature of their work, and the level of suffering that they may well have endured before their execution. Buckmaster did not fully explain the subtleties that surrounded the process of sending agents into the field.

Failure to inform relatives of the fate of agents within a reasonable time span was the least of French Section's concerns, since the whole Section had been responsible for far more serious and deadly mistakes. Although, according to government officials, there were mitigating circumstances:

> Buckmaster would have had to rely on accurate work by a number of other people before the signal from the agent physically reached him. It would have passed through the radio clerks who received the messages, the decoding clerks, and also his signals section for interpretation and advice if there was any suspicious indication in a message that might suggest enemy control. There were many changes in the staff involved with the above mentioned work and continuity and experience

were lacking. Buckmaster saw all messages that came in from France but he saw the finished article, i.e. the signal itself. If the security checks were not present there was a stamp on the signal 'security codes absent.' There was, however, quite a wide field for error in the form and contents of the message after it was received in England and before it reached Buckmaster.[4]

Nevertheless, this official view did not exonerate the leader of French Section and, while it was laudable for Buckmaster and his colleagues to try to protect and defend the reputation of their unit, some allegations were impossible to dispel. For instance, there was irrefutable evidence that agents' radio networks had been penetrated by the Abwehr. London was aware of this security breach yet continued to send agents into the field. Some agents had been foolish enough not even to use a code when transmitting information to London. This dangerous oversight, and others, naturally gave rise to criticism of amateurish SOE training and behaviour, though Buckmaster argued convincingly that the SOE was no more amateurish than the Special Air Service and other units that were established in wartime.

Perhaps the most appalling accusation made against us is that we deliberately sent our agents into the hands of the Germans. It is inferred that we did this to distract the attention of the Germans from the operations of other 'more important' organisations. This, it is said, was deliberately concealed by us from the public. I flatly deny these monstrous and intolerable accusations and challenge anyone to substantiate them. Indeed, I strongly deplore the efforts of these writers to discredit the achievements of the agents who worked for the French Section of SOE, and the officers in London responsible for the conduct of operations.

SOE, I must stress was NOT an espionage organisation. It operated militarily under the direct command of the SHAEF [Supreme Headquarters Allied Expeditionary Force] organisation, of which General Eisenhower was appointed commander. Its directives were received from the Ministry of Economic Warfare and SHAEF. It contained a number of people eminent in their various ways. Some were in uniform, some were in civilian clothes. Some were officers of the Regular Army, Navy and Air Force: others were specialists in a multiplicity of jobs in civilian life. All were imbued with one spirit only – to contribute to the maximum of their ability towards winning the war in the shortest possible time. The French Section headquarters staff was no exception. It contained, among others, a journalist, a chartered accountant, a wine merchant and a banker. All had one thing in common – a burning love for France and a high sense of duty.[5]

Buckmaster was actually on a pretty firm footing when extolling the virtues of his organisation at this point in his career, because SOE files were closed to the public. Evidence from across the Channel, however, continued to act as a thorn in his side. Members of the Resistance and the organisers of German counter-espionage circuits systematically exposed what became known as the 'radio game'. One particularly damaging account of the 'radio game' had been published by the previous head of German counter-espionage in Holland five years earlier. Responding to his revelations and questions in Parliament, Anthony Eden, the then Foreign Secretary, had been forced to acknowledge that much of the account was true. Buckmaster, nevertheless, was loath to admit that any parallels could be drawn between the French situation and that of Holland and Belgium.

Fuelled by a constant stream of revelations from across the Channel, Buckmaster blustered and brazened at the accusations that were now being fired thick and fast in his direction. Odette took a more pragmatic approach to the rising political storm and confessed to a reporter:

> You might be right about amateurs. We had some strange English people with us. One man came to me in a French village. He had a pipe and a tweed jacket. He looked terribly English. The next day the whole village was saying, 'Have you seen the Englishman?' But I will tell you that this same man did tremendous things and has a wonderful record. You do not know of these things because not everyone could be mentioned. Isn't that perhaps the reason for the new controversy that has arisen?[6]

For his part, Peter Churchill decided to ask the French government to conduct their own investigation into the work of British undercover agents on their territory. By this stage, the French newspaper reporters were also having a field day and conspiracy theories relating to the SOE were being published on an almost daily basis. There appeared to be no port in a storm for former SOE members, despite the fact that, as Buckmaster was fond of pointing out:

> Let us make no mistake about the importance which the Germans themselves attached to the activities of French Section. I have seen a sworn document under trial after the war, which emphasises in unmistakable terms that the Berlin Security Headquarters regarded the French Section as their number one enemy!

The French Section of SOE was not, of course, the only organisation in the field in France and the total effect of the French Resistance, in the words of General Eisenhower, 'shortened the war by nine months.' The opinions of my military chiefs have been expressed in citations for awards from British, American and French governments to the officers of French Section. The world owes to the men and women who worked for the Section a debt which can never be fully discharged, but those who mourn them can console themselves in the thought that their sacrifice was not in vain. Their grief will not be lightened by misguided attempts to show the contrary.[7]

But clearly the SOE was an espionage organisation, and despite Buckmaster's firm assertions and blustering rhetoric, official documents that were shielded from public view revealed a harrowing truth:

The Germans were able, apparently for some months, at the end of 1943 and in the spring of 1944 to play back to F Section H.Q. at least four radios which they had captured from F Section agents in France. F Section in due course spotted the German game but in the meantime tons of expensive arms and explosives and, more important still, agents, had been delivered to enemy controlled circuits and therefore straight into German hands.[8]

Not surprisingly, government officials looked for reasons to explain French Section's glaring failures. The training of agents was rigorous and strenuous and no fault could be found in this area. Logically, therefore, the agent selection procedures came under increased scrutiny and it was clear that Buckmaster had chosen to override the recommendation of the training schools in several instances:

> Candidates for F Section were garnered in from all sorts of sources and they were interviewed firstly by a Staff Captain at French Section H.Q. whose recommendation was subsequently discussed by Buckmaster with his junior officers who probably interviewed the individual again. Buckmaster therefore does seem to have played a responsible part in the selection of the officers for F Section, but I think it must be said in fairness to him that it was not by any means easy to get the right staff during the war having regard to many other competing claims of other services. Buckmaster himself seems to have intervened in the final selection of the F Section agents to be sent to France.[9]

Whatever his personal strengths and failings Buckmaster published his own version of SOE operations in France called *They Fought Alone*. This version argued that the collapse of the Prosper circuit had no effect on French Section because there were two shadow organisations ready to step into the breach and take over the circuit's work. This was, in part, wishful thinking, since the collapse of Prosper had a devastating effect on the undercover work in France.[10]

As the public speculated about the growing web of deceit, an appeal to public sympathy on a grand scale had little effect on the weight of criticism that was mounting against the SOE. Indeed, the tide of publicity had turned and everybody associated with the organisation was under suspicion, including the nation's darling spy. SOE officials closed ranks in the hope that the criticism would eventually subside. Buckmaster had done his best to limit the damage of French Section failures but the whitewashing of certain operational calamities had deepened public distrust. The net of suspicion gradually widened to include individual agents, as government ministers, journalists and the public alike clamoured for the truth behind SOE cover-ups. The situation was further fuelled by French newspaper articles, and the controversy refused to go away. With the exception of Dame Irene Ward, British politicians generally adopted the view that French press reports should be ignored.

But for Odette, the negative publicity was about to become unbearable as an extremely vindictive campaign was launched by Dame Irene Ward to have her George Cross Award rescinded. Odette entered a phase of her life that she later described as more distressing than her experience in Ravensbrück. Her sense of duty and honour was now in question and she was forced to defend her reputation.

Notes

1 The National Archives Treasury Files: TS58/1160. This file deals with the financial implications of a possible libel case associated with the publication of the official history of the SOE by M.D. Foot. The contents of this file are fascinating, and emphasise the missing sections of Odette's file. They also shed considerable light on how SOE women were viewed by the publisher and author of its official history.

2 *The Times*, 1 December 1958, p. 6.

3 *Daily Mirror*, 1 December 1958, newspaper cutting in The National Archives file: TS58/1160.

4 The National Archives Cabinet Papers: CAB 103/573, file ref: H69/94 part 3.

5 *Daily Mirror*, 1 December 1958, p. 6.

6 *The Sunday Dispatch*, 30 November 1958.

7 *Daily Mirror*, 1 December 1958, newspaper cutting in The National Archives file: TS58/1160.

8 The National Archives Cabinet Papers: CAB 103/573, file ref: H69/94 part 3.

9 *Ibid.*

10 *Ibid.*

16

FALLEN HEROINE

Throughout the late 1950s and early 1960s an increasing number of people crawled out of the woodwork to attack the SOE. Recent negative publicity had clearly encouraged anyone with the slightest grudge against the organisation to jump on the publicity bandwagon. Some, of course, had genuine grievances, but there were others who were simply throwing in their gripes for good measure in the hope of attracting attention. There was also a shift in media focus. Criticisms levelled at the organisation as a whole were gradually replaced by criticisms levelled at individual SOE agents.

To some extent this process represented a normal publicity backlash. Historically the British press were in the habit of extolling the virtues of heroes and heroines one minute and then knocking them off their pedestal the next. In Australia this process was called the 'tall poppy syndrome', a peculiar feature of all societies, where nobody was allowed to be considered better than the rest of the population for too long since heroic people made the rest feel inadequate. But the accusations that were now being generated against former agents went beyond this normal 'backlash' phenomenon. For those who exerted authority within the SOE, such as Buckmaster and Selwyn Jepson, the shifting of attention away from the organisation and onto the agents themselves was a welcome relief. The bulk of critical press coverage however, was largely directed at the most celebrated of SOE agents, Odette, and at her ex-husband, Peter Churchill.

Given her wartime ordeals and her exemplary courage it is difficult in many respects to explain why Odette suddenly became the subject of vitriolic publicity campaigns, all of which were littered with ridiculous accusations and sinister innuendo. Certainly in a patriarchal society there was a gender bias in some of the articles published. During the war, many men had broken down and given away information to the Germans under the pressure of Gestapo torture, and it was no doubt embarrassing for some men to acknowledge that SOE women had been braver in the face of such torture. After the war, government officials had tried to persuade all women to return to home and hearth, arguing that their rightful place was in the kitchen. The BBC introduced 'Women's Hour' to entertain women once they had completed their morning's housework, and popular women's magazines ran a 'Beauty is your Duty' campaign, suggesting that all wives and girlfriends had a duty to look ravishing for their husbands and boyfriends, especially those returning from military duty. Even popular songs such as 'Keep Young and Beautiful if you want to be Loved' pressed home the traditional role of women.

There was no doubt that films about SOE women inspired the sense of the heroic in women, and in the 1950s this was not the desired political message. It is also likely that men, and SOE men in particular, did not want to be reminded of how female agents were treated by the Gestapo. This prevailing attitude was indicated by the failure to show torture techniques in the celluloid depictions of their SOE careers. The Gestapo treatment of female agents differed considerably from that of male agents. The interrogation of women included torture techniques that were far more sexual in nature. This was a fact that male members of a patriarchal society did not want to consider in any great detail. Thus at this time, there were claims from male government ministers, military officials, journalists and academics alike that descriptions of female torture at the hands of the Gestapo had all been grossly exaggerated.

The press persecution of Odette, however, had far more sinister overtones. In view of the fact that she had signed an affidavit that firmly accused certain people in high authority of being double agents, she had become an inconvenient survivor. Although bound by the Official Secrets Act, it was evident that Odette possessed information that could severely damage the reputation, careers and lives of others. The inexplicable disappearance of the signed affidavit and certain other documents from her personnel file suggest that someone, somewhere in the SOE, was destroying evidence. It can also be argued that Odette's reputation was deliberately being tarnished by people who wished to protect their own. What better way for a double agent to protect himself than by casting doubt on the integrity of the person who could identify and testify against him?

To this day the signed affidavit that accused some of those high up in the SOE of spying for the Germans has not been found. Furthermore, in the late 1950s, official documents that had been buried in SOE vaults for years suddenly resurfaced without explanation. For instance, in 1950 six members of the French Resistance signed a protest letter which criticised the work conduct of both Odette and her then husband Peter Churchill, and argued that they were both being given undue credit for their undercover activities; this same letter mysteriously surfaced in 1958 to be published by the national press. The letter was also published in Paris, as France launched its own official inquiry into the Anglo-French activities of the Resistance movement.

The specific accusations levelled at Odette were threefold. Firstly, she was accused of telling lies about her torture and internment experiences. Secondly, it was claimed that she had survived Ravensbrück because she had embarked on an affair with the camp Commandant Fritz Suhren, and thirdly, that her undercover work in the field had not achieved the desired results because she had spent most of her time in bed with her commanding officer.

To begin with Odette did not even bother to refute the accusations, since she considered them too ridiculous to be believed. But a concerted effort to undermine her reputation appeared to be under way on both sides of the Channel. French reporters made much more of the accusations than did their British counterparts, perhaps because of the impending investigation. The decision taken by General de Gaulle to launch an official Anglo-French inquiry had made several ex-Resistance members and SOE officials apprehensive. Claims and counter-claims with regard to undercover operations were played out at length within official and unofficial circles. Ironically, the British press were outraged by the French accusations being levelled at Odette and gave the heroine a chance to answer her critics. Signatories of the newly resurfaced French protest letter had asked for proof of at least one act of sabotage, hostility or damage that had been initiated by Odette or Peter Churchill. The *Daily Telegraph* headline thundered:

ODETTE G.C. AND A FRENCH ATTACK

She [Odette] pointed out that the six men who were making the attack had waited thirteen years before doing so. 'I know why,' she said. 'They are uneasy. And the three men concerned in this thing whose names I know all had a grudge against Peter Churchill. I was not a saboteur, so of course I did no sabotage. I did my job as a courier and it was for that I got my M.B.E. The George Cross was for my time in captivity.'[1]

The signatories of the protest letter included Girard, Captain Bazin and De Malval. Two of these three were referred to in Odette's personnel file, and she had suspected the latter of having pocketed some of the Resistance funds.

> Girard was head of a French resistance group working with Peter Churchill. His men wanted him removed and went to Peter about it. Because it was a sort of domestic matter Peter would not interfere. Girard failed to get a vote of confidence from his men and was sent to England and then on to America. Bazin I have never met. He was working in Cannes before I got there and was considered very unreliable in his work. Certain steps were taken about him presumably by Peter Churchill. De Malval was never a prominent person in the resistance. He was a good French patriot, but he would not have known anything much and never did anything terribly important. After the war he felt that he had not had the recognition he deserved.[2]

From across the other side of the Channel, a reporter for the same newspaper interviewed Captain Bazin in Paris:

> We are not in any way questioning Churchill's or Odette's bravery or courage. Their contribution has to be seen in

its proper perspective. There are also things in their books which we think had better been kept secret.

Asked about the document he replied: 'Its all old stuff. I first learned that it had been made public this morning when my son-in-law called to me from London.'[3]

A *Daily Express* reporter also interviewed Bazin that evening, and the former Resistance leader seemed genuinely confused about all the fuss:

I just can't understand it. We signed that document in 1950. I am mystified that it should now come to light so late.[4]

The *Daily Telegraph* reporter travelled to Le Rouret near Grasse and asked Peter Churchill for his views. Speaking about his ex-wife he maintained:

I have never known such a brave woman. She is an international heroine who faced every imaginable danger. She never shrank from any kind of danger. The reply to criticisms of me can be found in my three books where I have tried to set down the truth.[5]

The controversy over the hotly disputed claims of ex-Resistance fighters continued to play out in the press over the following weeks. Odette remained aloof and diplomatic in the face of accusations; Peter Churchill, however, incensed at the injustice of the challenges laid down in the letter, took a more aggressive stance and faced the deluge head on. Ten days after the protest letter was first publicised the *Daily Mail* reported:

Wartime cloak and dagger hero Captain Peter Churchill yesterday answered one of the six men who have challenged him and his ex-wife Odette, to prove that they performed one single act of sabotage against the enemy. Captain Churchill, now a greying fifty year old said simply: 'My first job in France was to organise the escape of Captain Francis Bazin – this man who now puts his name to a damp squib of a challenge. He was being held in France in 1942. Everything was arranged to winkle him off the train as he travelled across France to a P.O.W. camp. I was liaising with the French Resistance and we got four men on the train. They gave Captain Bazin the Maquis signal, indicating that everything was laid on for an escape. But Bazin waved his head in a negative way, which was taken to mean that he did not want to be liberated. I never knew why.'[6]

Bazin's replies to Churchill's assertions were also reported at length and a battle of words turned into a full-scale war as Bazin claimed:

Peter Churchill had absolutely nothing whatever to do with the attempt to rescue me. The facts of my case are these: my friends from my section of the Underground organised the attempt to free me. There were three gendarmes in my compartment guarding me and another prisoner. We were handcuffed together. That was why when my friends gave the signal that they were ready to move I gave them the signal not to try anything.[7]

Peter Churchill, meanwhile, dismissed Bazin's claims as half-cocked, envious and sordid.[8]

This long-running war of words had successfully detracted attention from the overall administration of the SOE. Moreover, it is highly probable that the protest letter that had remained quietly hidden for eight years had been resurrected in a calculated manner by someone for just such a purpose. Certainly nobody claimed responsibility for its magical reappearance. Speaking from his home in Paris, Bazin suggested that the letter may have been brought into the public domain by one of the other signatories, but there was no proof that this was the case.

Back in London, Odette tried to weather the storm of controversy by playing down the significance of the disgruntled ex-Resistance men.

> They should have kept quiet. They are bringing into the open things that they know little about.[9]

But ex-Resistance members were slow to retreat into the shadows of obscurity; and several pointed out that hundreds of other British and French officers had done far more than Odette and her former commanding officer to further the war effort yet they had not received anywhere near the same notoriety. There were even some who believed that Odette had done little to warrant her MBE, George Cross and *Légion d'honneur*. To his credit, Peter Churchill was always quick to defend his ex-wife:

> It is the most amazing accusation ever made. We may be divorced, but I can still say that but for Odette's courage under torture hundreds of others would have been arrested by the Gestapo.

> I don't think that I was any great shakes in the Resistance.
> Luck enabled me to fulfil my missions.[10]

Buckmaster also joined the fray and spoke out in defence of
his two famous agents.

> It is quite monstrous that anyone should make this kind of
> attack on Peter Churchill or Odette.
>
> Odette's activities were unspectacular, necessarily so. If
> they had not been unspectacular she would have been no
> good. She did her job impeccably.
>
> What Churchill did must still largely remain secret, but his
> work in the reconnoitring of means of landing secret agents
> in France was invaluable and made an entire difference
> to our operations. That alone would have justified all
> the decorations.[11]

The endorsement of her former husband and commanding
officer, along with that of Buckmaster, temporarily gave
Odette some respite from the unremittingly negative press
attention. But worse was to come. Dame Irene Ward, who
had tabled the original motion in the House of Commons
demanding a full inquiry into SOE activities, turned her
attention towards the increasingly beleaguered Odette. The
public may have been appeased by official statements that
confirmed her impeccable work record, but Ward was not.
As far as she was concerned, there were still a number of
very awkward questions that needed to be answered by
SOE officials, and in the absence of answers Ward embarked
on a concerted and vitriolic campaign that was designed
to strip Odette of her George Cross medal and destroy
her reputation.

Notes

1 *Daily Telegraph*, 24 November 1958.
2 *Ibid.*
3 *Ibid.*
4 *Daily Express*, 24 November 1958.
5 *Daily Telegraph*, 24 November 1958.
6 *Daily Mail*, 4 December 1958.
7 *Ibid.*
8 *Ibid.*
9 *Daily Express*, 24 November 1958.
10 *Ibid.*
11 *Daily Telegraph*, 24 November 1958.

17

THE WARD VENDETTA

There was no doubt that Dame Irene Ward had decided to push for a full investigation into the effectiveness of the SOE, primarily because of the accusations and revelations that were contained in the books of Jean Overton-Fuller and Elizabeth Nicholas. These publications had sparked a series of other controversial works and public speculation had gathered momentum.

The well-researched central character in Jean Overton-Fuller's book was a French pilot who had been recruited by French Section and returned to France to work as an undercover agent. His subsequent activities revealed him to be a double agent. There was no official government response to the subject of the SOE storyline, but clearly such an agent existed. Indeed, he was tried and acquitted by a French court at the end of the war. Odette recalled the man in question at the time, but could only hint at the possibility of his being a double agent:

> I know this man referred to, I know him very well. But as my wartime superiors and the government have said nothing, I can say nothing.[1]

Of course, Odette knew a lot more about double agents than she was able, under the Official Secrets Act, to reveal. When fighting to protect her own reputation and those of her loyal comrades, she was metaphorically fighting with one arm tied behind her back. Speaking of Dame Irene Ward's request for a full investigation into SOE activities Odette, yet again, was diplomatic:

> I understand why she did it, but it is a pity in a way. The reputations and memories of so many who gave their families or their lives are being tarnished for one or two who did not do the right thing.[2]

Buckmaster did his best to placate the media and gave an official press statement justifying the actions of French Section.

Dame Ward, meanwhile, attempted to sieze the moral high ground with regard to her mission:

> I have no comment to make on the statement in view of the fact that I am in touch with the Prime Minister and the Foreign Secretary on the matter.[3]

While Odette was naturally adept at the art of tact, subtlety and diplomacy, these traits did not feature strongly in the character of Dame Irene Ward. Furthermore, the latter had no intention of restricting her suspicions and investigations merely to the administration of the SOE. As far as Ward was concerned, all undercover agents and their wartime records were under suspicion. In fact, Ward's subsequent behaviour could be likened to the proverbial bull in a china shop. Without any evidence to substantiate her claims, she publicly denounced Odette as a phoney. Then, with a combination of bigotry, ignorance and political verbosity she embarked on a lengthy and scathing vendetta that was designed to undermine the heroine on every level. Ward was not going to be satisfied with anything short of a comprehensive character assassination. As she patiently and stoically faced the onslaught, Odette pointed out:

> The idol topplers are at work. There is even one person who wants me to prove that I was tortured, that the Nazis drew my toe nails out, that my suffering was as I said it was. I have been turned into a kind of post-war Joan of Arc. It is not my fault that this has happened. Should I now have to prove myself? Is not the citation of the Government that gave me the George Cross good enough? The day has arrived when people are asking: Why is she, Odette, the only one of the women agents condemned to death who is still alive?[4]

In compiling her case against the heroine, Ward had revisited a number of rumours and insinuations with regard to the circumstances of Odette's arrest, torture and survival. She latched on to Hugo Bleicher's spurious claim that Odette was found in bed with her commanding officer when the couple were arrested. Bleicher was a man scorned by Odette and it was not surprising that he chose to embellish his account.

The British public did not seem unduly worried about this claim; the circumstances of the arrest were irrelevant. Odette and Peter Churchill had been working as man and wife because this was part of their cover story in the field. If anything, the fact that they had fallen in love actually strengthened their cover and enabled them to operate more freely. Although Odette was arrested in the hall of the Cottets' hotel, a few minutes later she probably would have been in bed with Peter.

Much to the chagrin of Ward, the British press seemed to skirt over her accusations against Odette. With the advent of an official French investigation into the work of Resistance movements, it was the French media that delighted more in highlighting the couple's affair, perhaps to shed a more favourable light on the work of French patriots and detract attention from the efforts of the SOE.

Not content with casting aspersions on the circumstances of the arrest, Ward accused Odette of exaggerating her accounts of torture. Odette had recounted her experience of having her toenails pulled out during her post-war debriefing interrogation. However, over a third of her interrogation statement had mysteriously disappeared from her personnel file, along with the affidavit; and it was the missing section of the statement that contained the graphic account of her torture. From an official point of view, therefore, Odette could not verify her story. It was not even possible to obtain proof from the man who had conducted the torture because he had been shot dead at the end of the war. Substantial medical evidence, however, did support Odette's version of events. It took three years for her toenails to grow back, and a medical officer confirmed in writing that they had indeed been ripped from their nail beds.

By now, Ward's attempt to get British public support for her campaign was faltering. She made a further attempt to cast doubt on Odette's integrity by suggesting that the heroine had embarked on an affair with the Commandant of Ravensbrück in order to secure her survival. This particular slur on Odette's character did appear to gain some ground within French Section and, despite the lack of evidence, Selwyn Jepson was prone to repeat the slur as a matter of undisputed fact. However, Jepson's correspondence suggests that he was also a misogynist who disliked Odette intensely because she had spoken out about her experiences. He could never quite get to grips with the idea that women could display more strength in some circumstances than their male colleagues. Although Odette was encouraged by the War Office to speak about her torture and internment, Jepson believed that she had revealed too much about the SOE in doing so.

Obviously the very idea that Odette would embark on an affair with the man who had ordered the deaths of thousands of women, including her comrades, was ludicrous in the extreme. Even without knowing the stubborn, determined and wilful Odette, the evidence of her internment, such as it existed, did not in any way support such a claim. A survival photograph was taken at the time of her liberation and just a cursory glance at the gaunt, emaciated Odette with matted waist-length hair covered in scabies would have been enough for most people to realise that an affair had not been taking place. While it was true that Suhren had released Odette from her Ravensbrück bunker, he had done so in the hope of gaining some favour with Allied Command. Moreover, Odette had handed the Commandant over to American soldiers, without hesitation, as soon as they had reached the American lines. A liaison between Odette and the Commandant would have been out of the question; the suggestion was too ridiculous to contemplate. Clearly, Suhren had mistakenly believed that she was closely related to the Prime Minister and was, therefore, someone of great importance. Odette maintained at the time, and until her death, that she owed her survival to the name of Churchill.

Despite Ward's machinations, the British public were generally supportive of Odette. Some time earlier, Odette's George Cross and *Légion d'honneur* medals had been stolen and the press had reported the story with such outrage that the thief actually returned the medals two days later, wrapped in a cheap tobacco pouch accompanied by a note. The thief promised not to make a return visit and signed his apologetic note simply 'from a bad egg'. It seemed that the bulk of the British population were prepared to accept that the SOE might be guilty of suspect dealings, but not that their darling spy Odette could be guilty of any misdemeanour. Although Odette was born in France, the British had taken her to their hearts and there was no doubt that she had become a very British heroine. Ward had whispered her suspicions in the corridors of power, accused Odette in the media, but she had systematically failed to win public support for her character assassination. There was no doubt that this had been a particularly gruelling time for Odette. But during one low point, when serious aspersions were being cast in her direction, she was uplifted by a painter decorating her apartment, who assured her with a cheerful certainty:

Don't worry Miss, the country is behind you![5]

Odette also received letters and messages of support on a daily basis. Sustained by her own irrepressible sense of humour she simply continued with her life and tried to ignore the Ward campaign. Of course, it was true that she had fallen in love with her commanding officer but this fact had nothing to do with her subsequent heroism. Ward's accusations were simply unjust and all the more hurtful because they were coming from another woman. Odette had reasoned that men might have been intimidated by her bravery and silence in the face of the Gestapo, but she had expected more sympathy and appreciation from her own sex.

In her defence, it can be argued that Dame Irene Ward was determined to uncover the truth about SOE activities; nevertheless, she was somewhat blinkered in her views and approach to life. In addition to her series of unsubstantiated accusations and public disapproval of Odette, she had also indulged in some earnest correspondence with government officials, including Prime Minister Harold Macmillan and the Foreign Secretary. Fuelled by a sense of self-importance and moral outrage, Ward had chosen to pursue her vendetta at the highest level. She did not believe for one moment that Odette was a worthy recipient of the George Cross, and her preoccupation with her victim developed into something of an obsession. In fact, an examination of Ward's intense correspondence on the issue reveals a level of amusement, sarcasm and bewilderment on the part of government officials. They subsequently took great pains to placate Ward but were clearly mystified as to why a Member of Parliament should throw all her political energies into trying to rob a national heroine of her medals. A letter dated 8 May 1959 from Robert Knox to Sir Norman Brook pointed out that the George Cross could only be rescinded if the recipient had committed High Treason. To do so without reason would surely result in social instability and a lack of respect for the British government.[6]

In a similar vein, a letter from Sir Norman Brook to Mr Bligh on 1 June 1959 maintained:

There is no precedent to review gallantry awards, to do so would question the wisdom of the Sovereign's original decision to make the award.

There is also no possibility of taking French government to task for what is said in French newspapers which are not within their control.[7]

By 3 June the Prime Minister stepped into the fray and asserted in no uncertain terms that Ward was on a hiding to nothing in her attempt to strip Odette of her awards. Thus, a carefully worded, restrained but firm letter was sent to the indomitable MP on the subject:

Dear Irene

I have studied the enclosed documents, which you sent to me with your letter of May 6th. It would be a novel course to try and review, after an interval of 12 years, the grounds on which was made a recommendation to the Sovereign for a gallantry award. I do not think that there is any precedent for such a review – or any procedure for carrying it out. And, quite frankly I do not believe it could be satisfactorily done by any means short of a public enquiry – which you yourself admit would not be possible or desirable. I do not myself believe that the publication of such articles as those to which you drew my attention will do any substantial damage to our national reputation. I have no doubt that it would be a mistake to take any official note of them.

Yours Ever

Harold MacMillan.[8]

The Prime Minister had decided to take a 'least said soonest mended' approach to the French press while simultaneously adopting a firm line with Ward; but his pertinent comments were like water off a duck's back to the crusading MP. She refused to take the Prime Minister's views on board and continued to write her vindictive letters, but in a more heated fashion.

By this stage government officials were genuinely puzzled by Ward's continued persecution of Odette and were putting forward ideas and sentiments of their own. There were those who believed that perhaps Odette had inadvertently upset Ward in some way, whereas others took the view that Ward was probably objecting to Odette having the George Cross on the grounds that she was French. Finally, when all explanations seemed futile, Ward revealed her true colours. It was with some relief, therefore, when, following yet another of Ward's diatribes, Sir Norman Brook wrote to Mr Bligh on 10 June 1959:

> In this further letter Dame Irene Ward comes out into the open and admits that what really bothers her is that the George Cross should have been awarded to a woman who had a lover. This confirms my view that her representations afford no ground for reviewing the award, even if it were practicable to do so.[9]

Ward's vendetta was effectively over once she openly confessed her real objections to Odette's bravery awards. To argue that Odette's dangerous undercover work, her stoical silence under torture and her grim experiences in the notorious Ravensbrück concentration camp should be considered as nothing when compared with a simple act of adultery, was viewed within ministerial circles as quite simply ridiculous. The presence or absence of a lover in her life had absolutely no bearing whatsoever on Odette's brave conduct in the face of the enemy. Medals were awarded for courage and gallantry above and beyond the call of duty, and in this respect Odette fully deserved all her honours. Sensing defeat, Ward reluctantly retreated from her victim.

Eventually, the government decided that it was desirable to publish an official history of the SOE. This decision was seen by many as a victory for Ward's efforts to establish the truth about the organisation's activities. Certainly this is how Ward and her supporters viewed the decision. However, an examination of the War Office and other official documents pertaining to this period reveal that there were other more pressing justifications for an official history. Both the Americans and the Russians were, at this point in time, recording their own versions and accounts of their undercover wartime successes; naturally then, an official history of the SOE was infinitely desirable if British efforts were to be fully recognised and documented for posterity.

Notes

1   *Daily Telegraph*, 24 November 1958.
2   *Ibid.*
3   *Daily Telegraph*, 1 December 1958.
4   *The Sunday Dispatch*, 24 November 1958.
5   *Ibid.*
6   The National Archives: SOE Personnel Files, ref: T350/11.
7   *Ibid.*
8   *Ibid.*
9   *Ibid.*

18

THE OFFICIAL LINE

The task of providing the British public with an official, dispassionate and correct account of the history of the SOE was given to a young Oxford historian named Michael Foot. He was paid the princely sum of £1,800 per year for twenty-six months, a further £300 on completion and £600 for any subsequent work on the book that might be deemed necessary once the full draft was complete. The project began as a pilot study and, although the distinguished historian had access to many of the surviving SOE archives, his work was subjected to a good deal of scrutiny. The avenues of his research were also strictly curtailed.

> The oddest restriction was that: till it had been decided that this pilot study was to appear, much more importance had been attached to keeping the author out of the way of interested parties. But there was no uniformity. Some of those he was writing about knew what was happening, and could eventually make comments; others were kept completely in the dark.[1]

This restriction also extended to include the leader of French Section Colonel Buckmaster, who was naturally indignant:

> I cannot think that the ban imposed upon the author against meeting me and discussing the more obscure questions can have served either the interests of the historian or of the readers, and I regard it as an unmerited discourtesy.[2]

The government intended to squash the rumours that Nazi spies had been operating within the SOE once and for all. These rumours had been generated by the publication of Jean Overton-Fuller's book and were circulating with increasing intensity, both within official and public circles. The official line was that of course mistakes had been made during the course of SOE administration, but that these mistakes were common to all new organisations for which a blueprint had not existed prior to the outbreak of war. The fact that Foot was flatly denied access to certain agents and their recollections from the field naturally steered the historian towards a path of historical enquiry that would reach this foregone conclusion.

Bound by significant government restrictions, therefore, a somewhat distorted picture of SOE activities began to take shape as Foot meticulously sifted through the surviving documents. Some distortion was inevitable, given the fact that around eighty-five per cent of SOE files no longer existed when he embarked on his laborious project. Many of the files were destroyed in a fire at London headquarters just after the war, some went missing as a result of enemy action, and those that were held in the Cairo office were purposefully destroyed during the war to prevent them from falling into the hands of the German army. It can also be argued that, since agents' notes were often made under conditions of extreme duress, the documentation of some operations in no way represented a comprehensive or accurate account of events as they later transpired in the field.

This unavoidable inconsistency of evidence, when combined with the existing government restrictions, undoubtedly presented substantial obstacles to the committed historian. The lack of documentary evidence alone justified the need to seek out surviving agents and obtain their view points. Yet Foot was not given a free rein to pursue his research in this area. Signs that the historian was beginning to feel uneasy about his new role began to surface in April 1964. Referring to the forthcoming book, he admitted in a press interview:

> I am afraid that there will be a lot of red faces when it comes out, though probably mine will be the reddest.[3]

The possibility of corruption and distortion of facts by screening or otherwise falsifying records, by restricting access to certain individuals, or by simply guiding the historian onto well-established and politically expedient tracks of enquiry, had been carefully noted by some Members of Parliament. The Secretary of State for Foreign Affairs had previously given MPs the distinct impression that no restrictions whatsoever had been placed on the official historian's research efforts. In a written answer to one such concerned MP, Jackie Smyth on 11 May 1964, he gave the assurance that:

> Now that Her Majesty's government have decided in principle that it would be desirable for this work to be published, those who bore a significant share of responsibility for the operations in question must be given the opportunity

to read the draft history and to offer comments to the author in order to ensure that the work is as accurate and objective as possible. This will inevitably take some time and it is not possible therefore to indicate at present a possible date of publication.[4]

Odette was only one of a number of agents whose views were not consulted in the preparation of the book, despite the fact that she and her former commanding officer featured very heavily within the text. In fact, aside from her own SOE personnel files, the most interesting official documents dealing with Odette's life are those that are contained within the pages of Treasury records. In many respects the debates that were played out in the correspondence between Treasury officials, M.R.D. Foot and the prospective publishers with regard to Odette are highly amusing. They also display patronising views towards Odette's experiences and a collective level of condescension that is totally astonishing. A letter from Colonel Selwyn Jepson to the Treasury asserted that Odette was so keen to be a martyr that she ought to be tied to a bed post and whipped.[5]

The publishers held a strategy meeting on 23 September 1964 with the intention of pre-empting and forestalling possible libel actions. At this purposeful gathering, Sir Burke Trend read out a letter written by the Chairman of the Victoria Cross and George Cross Association, Sir John Smyth MP. This letter stated in no uncertain terms that Odette had expressed serious reservations to Smyth about the authenticity of the planned publication. A Treasury memorandum records:

It was decided that Mr Peter Wilkinson should ask General Gubbins to have another look at the passage about Odette. He was to be requested to give his opinion in writing whether Odette was likely to make trouble after publication.[6]

M.R.D. Foot's history of the SOE was designed to be a definitive history of the organisation and an official government publication. Publishers at Her Majesty's Stationery Office envisaged a global circulation and a high demand for the book, but officials at the Treasury were very concerned about the potential for libel action. The actions of some agents had been heavily criticised by Foot in his original text, and it seems that all those concerned with the book's publication were worried about precisely how much critical material they could get away with printing about individual agents without incurring legal action. For example, a passage of Foot's original text, galley proof 229, referring to Odette, claimed:

> Buckmaster affirmed to have been horrified when Odette was awarded the George Cross. He had recommended her only for the M.B.E. (which she got). He had no hand in drafting the citation for the George Cross. Odette was culpable of disobeying orders. So was Churchill. Sex took the upper hand with the known dismal results. They should both have been court martialled.[7]

The prospective publishers also noted that some of the text contained a nasty innuendo making the reader doubt whether her toe nails had actually been pulled out.[8]

This latter note was not really surprising. Foot had not seen all of Odette's interrogation documents because large sections were missing from her file. What is surprising, however, is the fact that all those concerned with the publication, except the Treasury, seemed to think that Odette might not take legal action to protect her reputation. This attitude was remarkably short-sighted to say the least.

Here was a woman who had been tortured and condemned to death by the Gestapo, interned in the notorious Ravensbrück camp and awarded the George Cross for her bravery; a woman who was prepared to stand up to the Gestapo was obviously likely to take legal steps to protect her good name. Amongst other things, the original text claimed that sensationalists had over-exaggerated the level of torture experienced by female SOE agents, and accused Odette of not being able to distinguish fact from fantasy. A letter dated 18 April 1966, and written to Lieutenant-Colonel Boxhall at the Foreign Office just ten days before the book was published, highlighted in some detail the overall Treasury concerns with regard to possible libel action. The missive was also highly critical of Foot's assumptions with regard to his damning indictment of Odette:

Dear Boxhall,

Many thanks for your letter of 15th April with your file 22666/A on Odette Sansom, together with the unregistered temporary folder. Thank you for flagging the documents for me. I shall be glad if you can confirm that the other files relating to Odette Sansom have disappeared.

I have been through Mr Foot's three notebooks, which I also return herewith, and can find no references in them to the Odette Sansom files, unless I have missed them. He must, however, have seen the files which I return herewith. It is unfortunate that part of the interrogation of Odette Sansom dated 12th May 1945, and the shorter interrogation of the same date, are incomplete. There has clearly been removed from the main document at folio 326, certain pages at the end. I do not know why or where these missing pages are. It is of some importance because

Foot says in his book that in her formal interrogation on her return she made no reference to this incident at all. I do not see how he can say this if he has not seen the whole of the interrogation. Admittedly, the reference to the removal of her toenails by the Nazis would have appeared at about the middle of the interrogation if it had been dealt with in the normal order. However, I feel that Counsel for Mrs Hallowes could make considerable play with this document as it stands at the present. Could you please find out where the rest of the interrogation is?

The other difficulty about the remaining documents is that the medical certificate AQ/MED to D/FIN 1 of 14th November 1945 which is quoted as the authority for saying that Odette Sansom for many months had difficulty distinguishing fantasy from reality, unfortunately does not contain words to this effect. Undoubtedly she was in a state of nervous tension and her symptoms were mainly psychological and disclosed no organic disease. This, however, is not the same as saying that she had difficulty in distinguishing fantasy from reality. I quite frankly do not know where Foot got these words from. They do not appear in Dr Markovitch's medical report of 31st May 1946. I have an uneasy feeling that they came from the last three lines of the annex to the Journal de la Villa Isabelle which of course is critical of Mrs Sansom and Peter Churchill.

There is nothing we can do about the text at this stage except, I suggest, to try and find the remaining and missing parts of the interrogation. The great difficulty about the story of the removal of the toenails, so far as we are concerned, will be in the citation for the George Cross which was signed by General Gubbins. Quite honestly, I do not see how he can go back on the views expressed in the citation which were, as I understand it, based on a recommendation signed by him. All the same, I cannot imagine that Mrs Hallowes would be advised to bring proceedings in respect of a possible innuendo ...[9]

Within the corridors of power, official discussion and frantic correspondence about Foot's flawed analysis continued to gather pace behind the scenes in the lead up to the long-awaited publication. But nobody seemed to realise that an attempt to portray Odette as a fantasist was a ridiculous notion. How could British government officials belatedly claim that she did not know fact from fantasy when the same government officials had asked her to give evidence and testify at the International War Crimes Tribunals? Odette was clear-headed when she gave evidence in Hamburg and her testimony was corroborated by other witnesses. Obviously she had been clear-headed enough to recall having her toenails removed by the Gestapo. It was not something that she was ever likely to forget, and it was certainly no fantasy. If Foot had been allowed reasonable access to interview surviving SOE agents, however, it is unlikely that he would have made such a foolish and offensive suggestion. As the MP Jackie Smyth asserted the day before publication:

It appears inconceivable to me that anyone like Odette Hallowes should have been precluded from seeing the draft at all. I hope that some of my colleagues in the House will elucidate from the Secretary of State for Foreign Affairs who exactly were shown the draft and whether these persons were selected by the author or by the Secretary of State.[10]

On the actual day of publication *The Times* editorial went a step further and stated:

The authorities were right to decide that the S.O.E. story should be told. They were right to engage a professional historian to tell it. They were wrong to keep Mr Foot on a lead, more suitable for a court poet than for someone who was supposed to be 'accurate and dispassionate.' He should have been told: 'These are the documents you can see; go ahead and make what you can of them and any other sources of information you can get hold of.' If this was impossible then it would have been better to have done nothing. The fact that Mr Foot has produced a very good book does not alter the argument. The faceless authorities will be encouraged to think that they can decide what shall be said as well as who shall say it. That is not history at all.[11]

Evidently there was considerable sympathy for the somewhat compromised Foot. Nevertheless, although he had courted the wrath of SOE agents by his unsympathetic and, at times, inaccurate portrayal of their activities and their characters, he had at least done his utmost to dispel the suggestion that agents had been deliberately dropped into enemy hands by Nazi spies who had infiltrated the SOE. Foot argued, though not convincingly, that these unfortunate occurrences were actually the result of administrative incompetence. He had reached a foregone conclusion that toed the official line admirably. But even if this were actually the case, it was a conclusion that was hardly reassuring for the British public. As a Cabinet Office memorandum pointed out:

To send agents knowingly to their doom seems impossible to justify and the book firmly therefore excludes this possibility. On the other hand Buckmaster must accept the disagreeable facts that many agents were sent by F Section to enemy controlled landing grounds owing to the captured radios being played back. If the agents were not dropped on purpose they were presumably dropped by mistake, and a mistake which arose out of the failure to detect German control in the wireless messages.[12]

The fact also remained that the affidavit which mysteriously disappeared from Odette's file had clearly cited men who she knew for certain to be double agents. These men were operational within French Section and never brought to account.

Members of the Cabinet appeared to be satisfied that the SOE book was a fair appraisal of operations. But the Treasury was still apprehensive about the possibility of litigation. The department was fairly confident of avoiding legal action in Britain, but was less convinced of surviving the wrath of the French. The French Resistance workers mentioned within the official text were likely to take action, and Treasury solicitors were not well acquainted with French law:

A particular problem arises in France, however, over the risk of legal proceedings for libel. This is because certain French agents, including some who broke down under enemy interrogation or went over to the other side, are mentioned by name and because under French law truthfulness is not a defence when the facts to which the defamation of character relates are more than ten years old. In addition, it is possible that some French agents who are 'libelled' in the book are covered by one or the other amnesties which have been granted since the war to persons involved with the Germans during the occupation; and it is an offence to refer to any matter covered by the amnesties.[13]

To ease the Treasury's worries, a French lawyer named Jerome Sauerwein was employed to explain the French legal minefield. Legal action was considered unlikely to ensue if the French government considered Foot's work to be serious history; but in the event, Sauerwein judged the book not to be a serious academic work. A letter from the Treasury solicitor to Colonel Boxhall explained the problem:

> [Sauerwein] agreed that there was no objection to a serious historical work based on available facts and historical data, but he stated that in his view, Mr Foot's book would not be regarded by the French Courts as a serious historical work, owing, I gather, to the style in which it is written. This in Sauerwin's opinion is more like a novel than a serious historical work, and to be fair, he did draw my attention to one of two examples of Mr Foot's work which perhaps open to criticism.[14]

In view of the libellous content of the book, Treasury solicitors had decided that it was necessary to obtain hefty indemnity insurances to cover both the British government and the historian against the possibility of litigation from across the Channel. Therefore, the official line had been maintained but only at some cost. Moreover, from the standpoint of individual agents, the official history of SOE French Section clearly fell into the genre that was frequently described by French pamphlets as *dans lequelle on me saurait faire la part de la realite et de la fiction.*[15]

Notes

1 *The Times*, 28 April 1966, p. 15.
2 The National Archives Cabinet Papers: CAB/103/573: Letter to Lt-Colonel Boxhall from Colonel Buckmaster dated 20 April 1965.
3 *The Times*, 27 April 1966, p. 13.
4 *Ibid.*
5 The National Archives Treasury File: TS58/1160.
6 *Ibid.*
7 *Ibid.*
8 *Ibid.*
9 The National Archives Treasury File: TS58/1160, letter ref: T. & M. 64/45/FNC dated 18 April 1966.
10 *The Times*, 27 April 1966, p. 13.
11 *The Times* editorial, 28 April 1966, p. 15.
12 The National Archives Cabinet Papers: CAB 103/573.
13 *Ibid.*
14 The National Archives: CAB 103/573, file memorandum T. & M. 64/45/FNC, letter from Treasury solicitor Charlton to Colonel Boxhall at the Foreign Office dated 18 June 1965.
15 *The Times Literary Supplement*, 11 March 1965.

19

THE APOLOGY

The official history of the *SOE in France* by M.R.D. Foot was published on 28 April 1966 and immediately prompted new controversy. This storm of public outrage was predictable since, given the restrictions that had hampered the author's research process, the overall text was not particularly balanced. It was possible to detect the extraordinarily skilled and understanding eye of the professional historian within the pages of the work, but the focus of analysis concentrated more on certain individuals rather than the government administration of the SOE. Thus its widespread publication shifted the focus of media attention neatly onto individual agents and their performances in the field. This unfair focus did not go unnoticed, and agents from a variety of countries expressed their discontent. Indeed, a few of these agents argued that their names and exploits should not have been mentioned at all, since enemies had long memories and lives were clearly endangered by the detailed publication of covert operations. However, by largely dismissing SOE administrative failings and concentrating on the mistakes of individual agents the book effectively took the heat off the government. Intentionally or inadvertently, the government and Foot had diverted attention from the possibility that the SOE had deliberately dropped agents into the hands of the enemy. Public speculation was being directed into more politically acceptable avenues of concern.

Odette received her personal copy of the SOE official history on the day of publication, the day of her fifty-fourth birthday. Up until this point she had not been consulted about the book or seen one word of the text that effectively questioned her personal integrity and military conduct. Odette's solicitors were quick to take action and issued a curt statement:

> Mrs Odette Hallowes GC, states that any impression conveyed that she has given an interview on the subject of Mr Foot's book is erroneous.[1]

This statement was followed by a letter to F.N. Charlton at the Treasury office dated 3 May 1966. The letter succinctly outlined Odette's concerns and the potential case for libel action.

> The situation is simple. In 1947 Mrs Hallowes, then Mrs Odette Churchill was presented with the George Cross for her behaviour as an agent in France both before and after her arrest. I know little or nothing of the details of the award except what must be common surmise that the government of the time thought she was worthy to receive it.
>
> The British government, i.e. the same government, in 1966, have under their authority caused a book to be published which leaves not a shadow of a doubt that its author and therefore by implication its sponsors regard Mrs Hallowes (as she is now) as unworthy of the award. But this is not stated in clear or honest terms but in some of the

most complicated double talk that I have had the misfortune to study for years.

For your delectation I cite a final passage reading: 'and it is neither charitable nor magnanimous to complain as some brave men and some vindictive gossips do that her George Cross should never have been given to her.'

It would require a cabalistic student to interpret this sentence but I do not think anyone reading it would be left with a shadow of doubt that a large number of people whose opinions count, i.e. brave men and presumably men whose bravery was demonstrated in S.O.E. regard Mrs Hallowes as unworthy of the George Cross.

It seems quite unnecessary to debate the issue of her worthiness. What is monstrous is that the government that gave it to her should now, by this kind of allusion and innuendo, seek to tell the whole world that it was mistaken. If evidence has emerged – and no one suggests it – to suggest that Mrs Hallowes obtained her award improperly then official action should be taken.[2]

Following on from the Dame Irene Ward vendetta these officially endorsed attacks on her character caused Odette considerable distress. As a renowned heroine she had lent her name to numerous charitable causes, and was also a member of the Victoria Cross and the George Cross Committee. Until her right to wear the George Cross was vindicated, however, she felt unable to wear the medal. Thus an extremely sensitive and very weary Odette withdrew from public life, while Lord Goodman of Goodman, Derrick and Co. solicitors endeavoured to secure justice for the heroine and an official apology.

The issues that Odette wanted resolved did not revolve around money. An overriding and innate sense of duty had always dictated Odette's behaviour with regard to her family and her work, and the fact that people were questioning her military record wounded her deeply. Officers such as Peter Churchill and Francis Cammaerts had described her conduct as exemplary but this was not reflected within the official history of the SOE. For the sake of her daughters, her comrades and future generations Odette needed to set the record straight. Nothing less than an official apology would suffice.

Peter Churchill was also much maligned within the pages of Foot's manuscript and he subsequently issued his own High Court libel action against the historian and the Government Stationery Office on 28 August. The historian responded churlishly by writing a curt letter to the Treasury, claiming that Peter Churchill was only taking legal action because he was, at that moment in time, experiencing financial difficulties and hoping to gain compensation money from the lawsuit. Elsewhere the book received mixed reviews. *The Times* pointed out its positive attributes and drew attention to the restrictions imposed on its author. Colonel Buckmaster claimed:

There are, however, few major factual misinterpretations, at least in my opinion; and rather tendentious and illogical deductions.[3]

Dame Irene Ward was insulted and accused the historian of being disingenuous because he had not acknowledged her help and advice in the preface of the book. As far as Ward was concerned, the book would never have been written had it not been for the questions she had raised about the SOE in the House of Commons – such was her personal belief in her own powers of persuasion. It did not occur to Ward for one minute that an official history was already being considered before she raised her concerns. Buckmaster, meanwhile, was seething with secret resentment at Odette, believing rightly or wrongly that his failings, and that of French Section, would not have been exposed at all if it were not for the press fascination with the heroine.[4]

Across the Channel the book elicited cautious praise from General Charles de Gaulle who wrote a personal letter to Foot on 11 May 1966.[5] De Gaulle had always been very wary of SOE operations in occupied France and viewed the presence of SOE agents as potential threat to political independence. As a result he was not particularly fond of members of the French Resistance who had worked with the SOE. French honours, therefore, were more likely to be conferred on those who had worked with the Free French Intelligence Service. The French public were not overly impressed with the activities of SOE agents either, and they were certainly not enamoured with the way the Resistance had been portrayed in subsequent British-made films. However, the fact that de Gaulle had bothered to write to Foot at all was perhaps some indication that he recognised the historian's attempt to give the French some of the credit they deserved. In contrast, Buckmaster was outraged at the sheer number of snide comments and character slurs that littered the pages of the official text. Writing to Lt Colonel Boxhall at the Foreign Office, he complained bitterly about the book:

On my return from abroad I heard deplorable accounts of television programmes and saw various highly undesirable press comments. I had foreseen these when I first wrote to you about the book, getting on for two years ago. I am aware of the author's readiness to retract or rectify some of the innuendos and I am pleased to know this, but I foresee another very unpleasant round of ill-informed comment and criticism in the press on the grounds that 'official' history should (whatever the qualifications of the word 'official' may be) state facts and only facts. I cannot begin to tell you what distress this book has brought to a number of my friends – a distress which not unnaturally they have vented on me.[6]

Buckmaster was not the only furious SOE veteran, and over the following weeks the hapless Foot received a steady stream of letters from disgruntled SOE personnel. However, none of the missives appeared to pierce the historian's ivory tower mentality. Academics were viewed by the general public as aloof, arrogant and set apart from the real world, and in some cases this view was totally justified. Acutely aware of the sensitive egos associated with the world of academia, a few reprimanding letters of protest were cautiously penned by other intellectuals. The most pertinent of these was a sensitively, intelligently and constructively written missive that was sent to Foot by Francis Cammaerts, the SOE officer whose life Odette had saved by her silence. The tone of the letter can be compared to that of a father praising his son for trying to do well and then gently chiding him for all the errors he has committed. Moreover, the content of the letter makes it perfectly clear that Foot had been seriously mistaken in many of his assumptions. While it is obvious that Cammaerts chose his words carefully to avoid affronting the undoubtedly sensitive ego of the official historian, he nevertheless revealed many of the gaping holes in his research.

Dear Mr Foot,

Now that I have had the pleasure to complete a careful reading of S.O.E. in France, I feel I must write to say that my first impression has been fully confirmed. I believe that you have achieved an astonishingly well balanced and clear picture, that the emphasis and balance is highly perceptive, and that, in the complex of emotions and hard feelings, you have threaded your way doing a remarkable task of evaluation.

I do hope, however, that this is a first edition, and that all concerned will assist you with facts, further documentation and, in some cases perhaps, certain other interpretations of situations which you may find helpful.

On documentation, I was a little surprised to see no mention of da Banouville, or the Sorbonne thesis on the history of the movement 'Combat'. A remarkable little thesis has also been published on the Corps Francs de Marseille by Madeline Baudouin. Pierre Raynaud has at his home some twenty-five scrap books with original documents and messages. Perhaps this kind of information could help you both with a completion of the bibliography and access to some of the original documents held privately.

I have, inevitably, a number of small items of minor corrections which mostly apply to my own experience. I did not get a hockey blue at Cambridge, and the Lysander in which I arrived did not take Frager back to London. I started with S.O.E. August 1st, 1942 (not October). The footnote about my citation for Odette is simply explained by the fact that both she and Rabinovitch had visited the Glises in Cannes. The S.O.E. film was called School for Danger. Gardener's clip broke, and was not unattached. It was not rash to light fires for a flare path in Hote Savoie.

It was easy, in many parts of France, to get by with a bad accent, and the 'Hotel de la Poste' at St Jorioz, where Churchill and Odette were arrested had actually been visited by Bleicher, who had his first long talk with her there. These are the sort of small details which may be useful – as perhaps my surprise that you use 'swashbuckling' to describe so modest and quiet a person as Roger Landes, and my doubt about patriotism being the main motivation of S.O.E. agents ...[7]

Cammaert's letter to Foot continued in a similar vein, patiently pointing out some of the more serious historical inaccuracies and fundamental research errors. The letter was lengthy and painstakingly accurate. As such, Treasury legal officials stored the correspondence as a crucial source of reference with regard to forthcoming libel action.

Francis Cammaerts had become Principal of Leicester Training College of Education after the war and was a highly intelligent man. His astute and sharp mind, combined with a meticulous attention to detail, had served him well as an agent in the field. He clearly suspected that Foot had been guided by civil service authorities to reach certain conclusions about the work of the SOE, and realised that a witch hunt of individual agents was a clever diversion. Working on the premise that the pen was mightier than the sword, Cammaerts had decided to do his utmost to rectify the plethora of historical research blunders by appealing to Foot as a fellow intellectual. Yet there was a strange satirical approach to the book within the academic world and official circles. Having previously stated that his face would be redder than everyone else's when the book was finally in print, Foot was now living up to his own prediction.

A steady flow of libel actions drifted into the Treasury offices with monotonous predictability during the following months. Foot, although unrepentant, was now in a gloomy mood and maintained that Peter Churchill, in particular, was only pursuing a libel action against him because he was short of money. This may well have been the case, but when Churchill had his day in court the judges found in his favour, and thousands of copies of *SOE in France* had to be recalled. Some were returned to the Treasury from as far away as Canada. Odette received compensation on 4 May 1966 to the tune of £646.

On 15 June 1966 Treasury officials reluctantly attended the offices of Goodman, Derrick and Co. to agree on certain amendments to the original text of *SOE in France*. The Treasury solicitor F.N. Charlton Esq. CB, CBE recorded:

A number of new amendments were suggested, all of which Mr Foot took note of and said that he would incorporate them in the reprint. The only new amendment which to me appeared dangerous was the one on pp. 251–252 which if Mrs Hallowes' version was accepted would put Colonel Buckmaster in an awkward position. I subsequently telephoned Mr Foot on the 16th June and warned him about the implications. The other new point which Mrs Hallowes mentioned was that she made an affidavit on her return after the war which accused certain people, though she was not specific who they were. (N.B. This shows her file is incomplete.)

Mrs Hallowes said that she did not feel able to wear the George Cross until her military conduct and right to wear the George Cross had been vindicated. She was a member of the Victoria Cross and George Cross Association who were having their banquet on the 12th July. She did not feel able to attend or wear her medal for the time being. She had told the Queen when she received it that she received it as a representative of many others worthier than she. Mrs Hallowes, who is a very competent and capable woman, is extremely sensitive about criticisms of her George Cross.[8]

Having claimed that the torture and treatment of female agents at the hands of the Gestapo had been grossly exaggerated by sensationmongers, M.R.D. Foot was being forced to backtrack. Odette had insisted that the historian make a full and public apology for his somewhat insensitive and crass remarks. Legal representatives of the Treasury also believed that a public apology was required, not only in order to appease Odette and the relatives of other female agents who had been tortured and executed by the Gestapo, but also to subdue the increasing level of public concern. Numerous accounts of how female agents were tortured were given at the War Crimes Tribunals, and it was outrageous to suggest that these accounts had been exaggerated. The grieving relatives of executed female agents were particularly appalled by Foot's apparent insensitivity. The historian, however, was far from contrite and in a letter to the Treasury solicitor dated 7 May 1966 he wrote:

Dear Charlton,

Here are the drafts I agreed to prepare this afternoon. I send copies by this post to Boxhall and McIndoe. I will be at home from about 5pm on Monday if you want me on the telephone. You will notice that in writing to *The Times* I propose to refer to Mrs Szabo as well as Mrs Hallowes. This may not best please the latter; but it seems to me to be if anything the more scandalous case of the two. It would never do to appear to be kow-towing to a millionaire's wife, while ignoring the affairs, which on the merits deserve equal treatment, of a junior secretary in a large firm. A further amendment to p. 431 will be necessary to cope with the reference to torture in Mrs Szabo's citation; but I don't trouble you with this immediately.

Yours

Michael Foot[9]

The tone of Foot's letter indicated a level of academic arrogance, a tinge of envy at the thought of Mr Hallowes' millions, and also a degree of astonishing ignorance. Odette had done her utmost since the end of the war to highlight the role played by her comrades in arms. Far from being displeased at the inclusion of Mrs Szabo in the public apology, Odette was proud to be associated with her brave comrade. Indeed, nothing pleased her more than to give due attention to the brave and beautiful women with whom she had served. Odette firmly believed that she had a duty to her fallen comrades to highlight their contribution to the war effort and ensure that their suffering and sacrifice was duly recognised. An official public apology was therefore crucial. Foot was reluctant to bend to the will of one woman, however. When the apology was eventually printed in *The Times* on 11 July 1966 it could hardly be described as heartfelt. It was a token admission of guilt rather than an act of contrition. The letter to the Editor stated:

Sir, There has been one major misunderstanding, among some minor ones, over my book on S.O.E. in France; it concerns awards of the George Cross to two women of exceptional gallantry, Mrs Odette Hallowes and Mrs Violette Szabo. I deeply regret that any references in the book have given rise to misunderstandings, and so caused keen distress to a very gallant officer. I never intended (as has been wrongly suggested in some quarters) to cast any doubt whatever on the worthiness of the G.C. awarded to Mrs Hallowes in 1946, and if any language of mine conveyed that impression, it was certainly never intended. It was equally never my intention to suggest that the late Mrs Szabo did not deserve her G.C.: quite the contrary. Here also, I deeply regret pain which has been caused to her daughter. In both cases I shall take the opportunity, in any reprinting of the book, to make my views quite clear.

I am, Sir, yours faithfully,

M.R.D. Foot[10]

It could be argued that Foot had already made his views perfectly clear. In the galley proof 229 of *SOE in France* the official historian had maintained that Tickell's book about Odette had been economical with the truth, but he was in no position to criticise. Francis Cammaerts had successfully exposed numerous research gaps and errors of historical analysis within his own account of the history of the SOE in France. Moreover, in view of the plethora of legal actions that were being taken out against the Government Stationery Office, Foot was given plenty of opportunity to clarify his views. In total, sixteen pages were rewritten and reprinted at a cost to the Treasury of £150. When all the media fuss and legal wrangling was over, public interest in the SOE eventually subsided. The official history of the *SOE in France* had served its purpose. Instead of asking why agents were dropped into enemy hands, the public had asked why certain agents had made errors of judgement in the field. As the Treasury solicitor Charlton had observed before the book even went to print:

Many of S.O.E. agents' mistakes in France which led to their arrest and the break up of their circuits are attributed in the book to faults in the personality of the agents and faulty training. It seems to me not only from the book but from what Buckmaster told me that there is little to criticise in the very strenuous training which the agents had to undergo after they had been originally selected.[11]

If SOE training and administration could not be criticised, then clearly the agents bore the brunt of the blame. Although, as Charlton also pointed out:

Buckmaster told me that the only satisfactory way of checking whether a circuit was controlled or not was by using an 'S' phone from an aircraft. He was and remains unconvinced by radio touch checks. It is reasonable I think to ask why the 'S' phone was not more often used … I consider that anyone reading the account of the radio game would come to the conclusion that Buckmaster and F Section were taken in by the Germans playing back captured radios … and furthermore were taken in for much longer periods than they ought to have been.[12]

Agents like Odette and Peter Churchill were simply convenient scapegoats for French Section's general incompetence. But they had successfully diverted public attention away from the more serious SOE failures and the possibility of enemy infiltration into its London headquarters.

Foot's first edition of the official history of *SOE in France* may have been a riveting read, but the agents concerned viewed the text as largely a work of fiction that failed to confront some deeply uncomfortable political issues.

Odette, however, did have the satisfaction of receiving a public apology, and she believed that she had set the record straight. Foot's dismissive attitude towards female agents and his cursory academic treatment of their exploits had backfired. It was clearly impossible for anyone to exaggerate the level of torture that Odette and her fellow comrades had experienced at the hands of the Gestapo.

Notes

1 *The Times*, 29 April 1966, p. 8.
2 The National Archives Treasury Files: TS58/1160.
3 The National Archives Cabinet Papers: CAB/103/573, lengthy memo dated 22 January 1965, referring to a discussion with Buckmaster where Buckmaster insists that problems with F Section would not have been publicised 'if press had not blown up story of Odette Sansom'. Memo also discusses the Foreign Office concerns about agents being unhappy with how they were being portrayed in the official history.
4 The National Archives Cabinet Papers: CAB/103/573, contains a number of letters from Dame Irene Ward to M.R.D. Foot with regard to the publication of his manuscript and her obvious disappointment and chagrin at not receiving a mention in the acknowledgements.
5 The National Archives Treasury Files: TS58/1157: Letter to M.R.D. Foot from Le General de Gaulle, 11 May 1966. My thanks are due to Dr Luc Berlivet for translating this letter, interpreting its contents and providing me with the French historical context in this respect.
6 The National Archives Treasury Files: TS58/1160.
7 The National Archives Treasury Files: TS58/1157, volume 2, letter to Mr M.R.D. Foot from Francis Cammaerts dated 24 May 1966.
8 The National Archives Treasury Files: TS58/1160. Memorandum ref: T. & M. 64/45/FNC, 15 June 1966.
9 The National Archives Treasury Files: TS58/1160. Letter to F.N. Charlton from M.R.D. Foot, 7 May 1966.
10 *The Times*, 11 July 1966, p. 13.
11 The National Archives Cabinet Papers: CAB 103/573.
12 *Ibid*.

20

REFLECTIONS

When reflecting on the course of her life in later years Odette continued to express generosity and forgiveness towards those who had persecuted her, both during and after the war. She also revealed her practical nature, recalling with some humour in 1985 that she still possessed the charcoal grey suit she had worn during her captivity:

> I chose a charcoal grey colour for my flannel suit before I left for France in 1942. When Vera Atkins asked me why I had chosen that colour, I told her, 'when I go to prison it will not show the dirt like black or a pale colour'. I didn't want to think that way but I always had an instinct you see – a feeling that I would be captured at some point. When I was in prison I turned the skirt an inch about each day so that it would not look too dirty. I wore it all through my captivity [laughs], and I still have it today.[1]

In 1985 Odette was asked, on reflection, whether she would ever consider entering into the realms of undercover work again, should another war break out. Her reply was an emphatic:

No – never! If there was another war and I could still stand
on my own two feet and do something then I would nurse,
I would cook, I would do anything else, but I would never
enter into that game again. It is very difficult to accept
some factors of that game. It (my life) has been fantastic.
I have seen people who are very evil, but because of this
I have also seen people who are very noble, people who
inspire me. I have been very lucky. I have a wonderful
family and I am a very happy woman with a marvellous
husband. People are most kind and generous to me, very
much more than I deserve. Every day I am touched by the
kindness of people.[2]

It was indicative of Odette's forgiving nature that she
described some of the misogynist men in the SOE as
being kind, intelligent and thoughtful. Even Colonel
Jepson, who had condescendingly written to the Treasury
claiming that she was trying to be a martyr, was described
as being a 'very kind man'. Furthermore, there was no hint
of regret or bitterness when she spoke of her captors and
tormentors. Aside from her courage, intelligence, humour,
spirit of generosity and integrity, the most remarkable
aspect of Odette's character was her enormous compassion
for those less fortunate than herself. Even through the
tumultuous years of the Ward vendetta and the SOE media
frenzy Odette never lost sight of the issues that were
close to her heart. Moreover, she strongly believed that
her own life experiences could be used for the benefit of
others. For instance, her distressing childhood experience
of poliomyelitis prompted her to support the National
Poliomyelitis Association in their successful endeavour to
develop a vaccine against the disease.[3] An avid and dynamic

member of numerous associations and committees, Odette became an ambassador for many causes.

But her post-war years were dogged by considerable pain, the result of a back injury sustained during her work as an undercover agent. Eventually, following a thorough medical assessment, she was registered permanently disabled as a result of her wartime internment. Thus the Foreign Office awarded her the sum of £1,360 for her suffering in Ravensbrück, and a disability pension of £413 per annum for life.[4]

In 1961, despite her own continued suffering, Odette threw herself wholeheartedly into campaigning for a newly formed human rights group. The now renowned Amnesty International was established in this year by a British lawyer named Peter Benenson, who had recognised the urgent need for a non-political organisation of human rights activists. In 1948 the United Nations had issued a Universal Declaration of Human Rights and stated that:

> All human beings are born free and equal in dignity and rights. They are endowed with reason and conscience and should act towards one another in the spirit of brotherhood. Everyone has the right to life, liberty and security of person. No one shall be subjected to torture or to cruel, inhuman or degrading treatment or punishment.[5]

While the UN declaration was laudable in its essence, torture continued to be a mainstream weapon in the arsenal of many governments across the globe. Political prisoners and people who were imprisoned for their religious beliefs constitute the bulk of those being tortured. Benenson set out to raise public awareness of human rights abuses, and made concerted efforts to protect and secure the release of the individuals concerned. As a previous victim of torture Odette was at the forefront of this endeavour. On 9 December 1961 *The Times* reported on Amnesty's symbolic candle of freedom:

> A candle surrounded by coils of barbed wire will burn for six hours on the porch of St Martin-in-the-Fields church tomorrow in remembrance of people throughout the world who are imprisoned for political or religious beliefs. It will be lit by Mrs Odette Hallowes after a service at 3pm in the crypt. Tomorrow has been appointed by the United Nations as Human Rights Day and special services will also be held in Birmingham, Plymouth, Oxford, Edinburgh and Bristol, organized by Amnesty, an international movement for freedom of opinion and religion.
>
> At St Martin's 60 senior Boy Scouts carrying the flags of the nations will form a guard of honour. Mr Carey Grant and Miss Julie Christie will appear publicly wearing handcuffs, a gesture which, according to Mr Peter Benenson, the Director of Amnesty, is designed to express shame at the 'countless numbers of human beings who are denied their freedom.' They will be released when the candle is lit. The church will be open for prayer all night.[6]

The symbolic candle of freedom surrounded by coils of barbed wire continued to be the symbol of Amnesty International and Odette enthusiastically supported the movement for the remainder of her life. As she reflected somewhat quietly and wistfully when interviewed:

> I have suffered but I have been so terribly fortunate – really, so incredibly fortunate. There are others who are still

suffering and enduring such dreadful conditions. I was a political prisoner and I know how things can be.[7]

In addition to her support of Amnesty International, Odette also took an active role in championing young air cadets within the Royal Air Force. This was her way of thanking the RAF for its role in supplying the French Resistance with arms and equipment, and thereby contributing to the liberation of her beloved homeland. She remembered with a deep sense of humble gratitude the human cost of their wartime missions, and in 1969 became the President of the East Ham 282 Squadron Air Training Corps. In subsequent conversations pertaining to the war years Odette always acknowledged the pilots who had played such a vital role in, what she referred to as, 'the wonderful RAF'.[8]

Odette's role with the RAF represented her own carefully orchestrated thank you mission, but a mere three years later she flew to Cannes on a mission of a more personal nature. Captain Peter Churchill, who had been living at Le Rouret on the French Riviera, was seriously ill and had been admitted to an English hospital in Cannes on 14 January 1972. Odette was one of the first to be at his bedside after admission.

A few months later, on 1 May 1972, Peter Churchill died at the relatively young age of sixty-three. His death marked the end of an era for Odette, who privately grieved his loss more than most. As her commanding officer Churchill had gained her loyalty, trust and respect. As a man he had gained her love and devotion. Regardless of the fact that their passionate love affair and subsequent marriage had floundered in the face of concerted media pressure, he had staunchly defended her reputation as a courageous heroine throughout the years of adverse publicity. Thus he remained her devoted friend to the end of his days.

But Odette was not a person prone to self-pity, and while she often reflected on the past she did not dwell on it. She counted her blessings and forever praised her husband Geoffrey Hallowes for his enduring love and devoted support. Her sense of humour continued to sustain her, and while the following years took their toll on Odette in a physical sense, her boundless mental vigour and moral fortitude remained constant. True to her word she never forgot her comrades in arms, and in May 1973 she established a special resting place for their stories and treasures. It was an attempt to place on record for future generations the spirit of those who had served their fellow citizens in the best possible manner. As *The Times* reported on 4 May 1973:

A company of some of the bravest men and women in Britain met at the Imperial War Museum yesterday to open a new room that will record and illustrate the history of the Victoria Cross and the George Cross. Each of them wore on the right of a chest loaded with decorations either a small blue ribbon and a silver cross or a crimson ribbon with a bronze Maltese cross made from the metal of two Russian cannon captured at Sebastopol. Opening the permanent exhibition, Rear Admiral Godfrey Place, V.C. said: 'Although a museum necessarily displays things, this exhibition also captures something of the way of life, and spirit and emotion of these people. I hope that it may be an influence on others in time of crisis to serve their fellow men in the tradition of the best in our civilisation.'

Next door to the exhibition a private room has been put at the disposal of members of the Victoria Cross and George Cross Association, where they can meet and keep their records and treasures. This room was the idea of Mrs Odette Hallowes, the comrade in danger and suffering of the 'white rabbit', Violette Szabo and others whose stories are told in the exhibition. She said: 'This is a fitting place for such a room, where we can meet each other and our overseas members when they come over for our reunions It is the right place eventually to keep our medals, otherwise they get lost or stolen. All of mine were stolen, but the press made such a fuss that the burglar sent them back with a very funny letter from South Kensington promising not to visit me again.'[9]

Odette always maintained that her fellow female SOE agents had suffered and committed acts of bravery that were far greater and more important than her own. Thus she took great pains to emphasise their role whenever it was possible to do so.

In a final and poignant homage to her fallen comrades, Odette returned to Ravensbrück in 1994 to unveil a memorial plaque in their honour. She had been liberated in 1945 and this was her first and only return visit to the camp. By now she was a frail eighty-one-year-old. But the memories and horrors of her brutal internment flooded back like an untamed torrential river. Near the carefully crafted memorial plaque the young, beautiful and vibrant faces of her comrades darted through her now aged mind. She pictured the serious, dignified face of Denise Bloch, the simple, elegant beauty of Violette Szabo and the glamorous distinctly attractive features of Lillian Rolfe. She visualised their smiles and their laughter. She remembered their determination and intelligence. She recalled their struggles, their torture and their grief at being captured. But most of all, with tears in her eyes, she remembered their outstanding bravery and ultimate sacrifice. This was an intensely moving and deeply profound emotional journey for Odette, now in her twilight years. Yet in many respects the journey represented a quiet completion of her turbulent and eventful life. The following year, on 13 March 1995, Odette passed away peacefully in her own bed in Walton-upon-Thames. The subsequent and numerous obituaries highlighted and praised her indomitable spirit and remarked on her lack of bitterness and forgiving nature. RAF 282 Squadron stated in its obituary:

Odette was a calm, thoughtful, lovely and generous person who never sought publicity; her faith and courage should never be forgotten by anybody in this generation or future generations. We salute a truly splendid person.[10]

It is perhaps fitting, however, to leave the last words of this biography to Odette herself. When asked about her beliefs, her faith, her life and her work, she replied with characteristic candour and sincerity:

I believe in the soul of people. I believe we all have a soul. We do not know where it comes from, what it is – or what it is made from; or what happens to it. But I believe that we have got to use it in the best possible way. I am a thousand years old but I love people, I really do. They are little miracles.[11]

Notes

1 Imperial War Museum, oral history interview with Odette Hallowes, 1985.
2 *Ibid*.
3 This charity has now been renamed Action Medical Research and it is still in the forefront of medical research. In recent years it has achieved remarkable successes and has been primarily associated with the treatment and improved survival rate of premature babies.
4 The National Archives: PIN93/1 claim file ref: c.46547.
5 United Nations Declaration of Human Rights articles 1, 3 and 5, 1948.
6 *The Times*, 9 December 1961, p. 4.
7 Imperial War Museum, oral history interview with Odette Hallowes, 1985.
8 Imperial War Museum, oral history interview with Odette Hallowes, 1985. Information also obtained from www.282squadron.org.uk.
9 *The Times*, 4 May 1973, p. 20.
10 www.282squadron.org.uk.
11 Imperial War Museum, oral history interview with Odette Hallowes, 1985.

Appendix I

AWARDING OF THE GEORGE CROSS

Central Chancery of the Orders of Knighthood, St James's Palace, London, SW1

20th August 1946

His Majesty the King has been graciously pleased to award the George Cross to:
Odette Marie Celine Sansom, M.B.E.
Women's Transport Service – First Aid Nursing Yeomanry.

Mrs Sansom was infiltrated into enemy occupied France and worked with great courage and distinction until April 1943, when she was arrested with her Commanding Officer. Between Marseilles and Paris on the way to the prison at Fresnes, she succeeded in speaking to her Commanding Officer and for mutual protection they agreed to maintain that they were married. She adhered to this story and even succeeded in convincing her captors in spite of considerable contrary evidence and through at least fourteen interrogations. She also drew Gestapo attention from her Commanding Officer on to herself saying that he had only come to France on her insistence. She took full responsibility and agreed that it should be herself and not her Commanding Officer who should be shot. By this action she caused the Gestapo to cease paying attention to her Commanding Officer after only two interrogations. In addition the Gestapo were most determined to discover the whereabouts of a wireless operator and of another British officer whose lives were of great value to the Resistance Organization. Mrs Sansom was the only person who knew of their whereabouts. The Gestapo tortured her most brutally to try to make her give away this information. They seared her back with a red hot iron and, when that failed, they pulled out all her toenails. Mrs Sansom however, continually refused to speak, and by her bravery and determination she not only saved the lives of the two officers but also enabled them to carry on their most valuable work. During the period of over two years in which she was in enemy hands, she displayed courage, endurance and self sacrifice of the highest possible order.

Appendix 2

RECOMMENDATION FOR MBE

Ensign Odette Sansom F.A.N.Y.

This Officer was landed in France by sea on the 2nd November 1942 as courier to an organiser in the South East, and worked for six months in dangerous and trying conditions. The circuit to which she was attached was large and widespread, and she travelled widely maintaining liaison between various groups, delivering operational messages and transporting wireless equipment. She was frequently stopped and searched by police and Gestapo and always showed outstanding coolness and complete contempt for danger. During March 1943, while her Commanding Officer was away on a visit to England, she took his place and proved herself a competent organiser. She arranged for several parachute deliveries of arms and equipment, and was always present on the reception ground to direct operations. She organised the reception of her Commanding Officer at very short notice and in a dangerous area, when he returned to France by parachute in early April. Ensign Sansom was arrested soon after this operation and spent more than two years in France and Germany before being repatriated to England in May 1945. For her courage, self sacrifice and devotion to duty it is recommended that this officer be awarded the Member of the British Empire.

Appendix 3

CHRONOLOGY OF EVENTS

1939

31 August: The British government issues orders to evacuate forthwith. As a result, over 3½ million men, women and children are evacuated from large urban cities to safer rural areas in preparation for war.

1 September: German forces invade Poland and Britain issues Germany with an ultimatum under the terms of the Anglo-Polish alliance.

3 September: Britain and France declare war on Germany.

17 September: Soviet troops enter Poland. (The USSR had signed a non-aggression pact with Germany, which was supposed to guarantee that Germany would not invade Soviet territory.)

28 September: Poland is divided by Germany and Russia.

30 November: The USSR invades Finland.

17 December: The last of the German pocket battleships, the *Graf Spee*, is scuttled at Montevideo on the orders of the German High Command. (This move was taken to avoid the embarrassing propaganda that would have ensued if the German population had found out that the ship had been severely damaged by the British Royal Navy during the Battle of the River Plate.)

1940

12 March: Peace Treaty is signed between the USSR and Finland.

9 April: German forces invade Denmark and Norway.

10 May: Germans invade Netherlands, Belgium and Luxembourg. Neville Chamberlain resigns and Winston Churchill takes his place as the British Prime Minister.

12 May: German forces cross the French border.

15 May: The Dutch army surrenders.

26 May – 4 June: The Dunkirk evacuation of British troops, during which nearly 900 ships, some in private ownership, ferry 338,226 troops from Dunkirk back to Britain.

28 May: King Leopold surrenders Belgium.

10 June: Italy enters the war on the side of Germany and declares war on Britain and France.

14 June: German forces take over Paris.

15 & 16 June: Russian forces capture Lithuania, Latvia and Estonia.

22 June: France and Germany sign an armistice.

10 July: Start of the Battle of Britain.

7 September: Start of the Blitz.

28 October: Italy invades Greece.

1941

10 January: America introduces a lend-lease policy into Congress, which offers financial support to Britain's war effort.

30 March: German forces mount a counter-offensive in North Africa.

6 April: Germany invades Greece and Yugoslavia.

11 April: The Russians sign a Neutrality Treaty with Japan.

20 May: German forces invade Crete.

1 June: The British withdraw from Crete.

8 June: British and Free French forces enter Syria.

14 June: President Roosevelt freezes German and Italian funds in America.

22 June: Germany invades Russia, ending the terms of the non-aggression pact.

12 July: Britain and Russia sign a mutual aid pact.

14 August: The Atlantic Charter: Roosevelt and Churchill meet at sea to discuss war aims.

25 August: British and Soviet troops enter Iran.

19 September: Germany captures Kiev.

11 October: General Tojo becomes Japan's premier.

18 November: The British Eighth Army begins a desert offensive in Libya.

28 November: Soviet forces recapture Rostov.

1 December: The Soviets stage a counter-offensive at Tula.

7 December: Japan attacks Pearl Harbor and destroys America's Pacific Fleet. Japan declares war on America and Britain.

8 December: Japanese forces land in Thailand and Malaya. America and Britain declare war on Japan.

9 December: Britain's HMS *Prince of Wales* and HMS *Repulse* are destroyed by Japanese aircraft off the coast of Malaya.

10 & 11 December: Germany and Italy declare war on America.

22 December: Japan begins major offensive in the Philippines, and Churchill attends the first Washington Conference.

25 December: Hong Kong surrenders to the Japanese.

1942

1 January: The United Nations Declaration is signed by twenty-six nations. (The Declaration effectively provided an alliance which pledged the military and economic support of the signatories against Germany and Italy. The Declaration also formed the basis of the United Nations Organisation, which was established after hostilities had ceased.)

10 & 11 January: Japanese forces invade the Dutch East Indies.

21 January: German forces stage a counter-offensive in North Africa.

15 February: Singapore falls to the Japanese. The British are forced to surrender the island.

7 March: The evacuation of Rangoon.

17 March: The American General MacArthur arrives in Australia to discuss Allied war aims in the Far East.

9 April: The American forces on Bataan surrender.

18 April: American aircraft launch bombing raids on Tokyo.

4 – 9 May: Battle of the Coral Sea.

26 May: Yet another German counter-offensive in North Africa.

30 – 31 May: The first Royal Air Force 'thousand bomber raid', under the command of Air Marshal Harris, takes place on Cologne.

4 June: Battle of Midway Island.

21 June: Germany captures Tobruk.

25 – 27 June: Second Washington Conference between Roosevelt and Churchill.

7 August: American forces land in Guadalcanal.

12 August: First Moscow Conference.

23 October: Montgomery strikes at El Alamein.

7 & 8 November: The Americans and British undertake a massive reinforcement of their troops in North Africa.

19 – 22 November: The Soviets stage a counter-offensive at Stalingrad.

1943

14 – 24 January: Casablanca Conference, attended by Churchill, Roosevelt and their Chiefs of Staff. Stalin does not attend, being preoccupied with military campaigns near Stalingrad.

23 January: The British Eighth Army enters Tripoli.

2 February: The German force surrenders at Stalingrad.

2 March: Battle of the Bismark Sea.

11 – 27 May: Third Washington Conference between Roosevelt and Churchill.

12 May: German and Italian resistance in Tunisia finishes.

18 May: United Nations Food Conference takes place in Virginia.

5 July: Battle of Kursk begins. (The Soviets eventually pushed back the Germans and were able to move onto the offensive along the whole of the Eastern Front. This battle signified a dramatic turning-point in the war in Europe.)

9 & 10 July: British and American forces invade Sicily.

19 July: Bombing raids begin on Rome.

25 July: Mussolini is replaced by Badogolio as Italy's premier.

17 – 24 August: First Quebec Conference, attended by Churchill, Roosevelt and their Chiefs of Staff; Stalin declines to attend.

3 September: British and American forces invade Italy.

8 September: Italy surrenders.

9 September: British and American forces land at Salerno.

10 September: German forces occupy Rome.

13 October: Italy declares war on Germany.

6 November: The Soviets recapture Kiev.

9 November: The United Nations Relief and Rehabilitation Administration is formed.

12 December: The Czecho-Soviet alliance is formed.

1944

22 January: British and American forces land behind German lines at Anzio.

8 March: The Finns reject the terms of the Russian armistice.

19 March: German forces cross the Hungarian border.

10 April: The Soviets retake Odessa.

23 May: British and American troops launch an offensive from Anzio beachhead.

4 June: Rome is captured by British and American troops.

6 June: D-Day: British and American invasion of Normandy.

13 & 14 June: The first V1 flying bombs (doodlebugs) land in Britain.

15 June: The first American B-29 Superfortress raid takes place on Japan.

3 July: The Soviets recapture Minsk.

27 July: American troops break through west of St Lô.

11 August: American forces occupy Guam.

15 August: British and American forces land on the French south coast.

25 August: Paris is liberated.

3 September: Brussels is liberated.

8 September: The first V2 rocket lands on London.

17 September: American and British troops land in Holland.

14 October: American and British forces occupy Athens.

20 October: Belgrade is liberated, and American troops invade the Philippines.

21 & 22 October: Battle of Leyte Gulf.

12 November: *Tirpitz* is sunk by the Royal Air Force.

16 December: The Germans launch their last major counter-offensive: the Battle of the Bulge.

1945

9 January: American forces land on Lozon in the Philippines.

11 January: The Soviets take Warsaw.

20 January: Hungary signs armistice.

27 January: Memel is liberated.

31 January: Churchill and Roosevelt meet at Malta.

3 February: American troops land at Manila.

4 – 12 February: Conference held at Yalta between Roosevelt, Stalin and Churchill.

19 February: American troops land on Iwo Jima.

7 March: The American First Army crosses the Rhine.

1 April: America invades Okinawa.

12 April: Roosevelt dies and is replaced as American President by Truman.

13 April: Vienna is liberated.

28 April: Mussolini is executed by partisan forces.

30 April: Hitler commits suicide in his bunker in Berlin; American forces liberate 33,000 inmates at Dachau concentration camp; and the Soviet flag is raised on the Reichstag in Berlin.

1 May: Admiral Dönitz assumes command of Germany.

2 May: Berlin falls to the Soviets.

3 May: Rangoon is captured.

7 May: Germany surrenders.

8 May: Victory in Europe Day.

17 July – 2 August: Potsdam Conference, attended by Churchill, Truman and Stalin.

6 August: Atomic bomb is dropped on Hiroshima.

8 August: The USSR declares war on Japan.

9 August: Second atomic bomb is dropped on Nagasaki.

14 August: Japan surrenders.

2 September: Japanese sign surrender terms in Tokyo Bay.

INDEX

Abwehr 76, 101, 102, 174
Amnesty International
    228–30
Annecy 94, 98, 100, 101, 103,
    106, 107, 109, 110, 121
Antwerp 135
Arnaud 69, 71, 78, 79, 93, 96,
    99, 100, 103, 107, 110, 113,
    121, 123, 168
Atkins, Vera 38, 40, 146, 147,
    165, 173, 226
Aufseherinnen 127
Aushwitz 149
Avenue Foch 10, 112–4, 119

Battle of Britain 28, 239
BBC 89, 90, 95–6, 106, 120,
    149, 181
Belsen 149
Binder, Gustav 152, 155
Binz, Dorothea 153, 155
Bleicher, Hugo (Henri) 102–7,
    113, 116–8, 192, 219
Bloch, Denise 120–2, 129,
    136, 166, 232

Boesel, Greta 155
Boulogne 20–1, 37
Brailly, Gaston 14–7
Brailly, Yvonne 14, 15, 18–22,
    29
Buckmaster, Maurice 38, 39,
    57–9, 62, 90, 98, 165,
    166, 171–8, 180, 188, 191,
    200, 204, 208, 211, 215–7,
    220, 224, 225

Calais 37
Cammaerts, Francis 98–9,
    101, 103, 110, 113, 121,
    160, 215, 217, 219, 223,
    225
CARTE network 66–8, 91–4,
    98–9
Chamberlain, Neville 25–7,
    239
Churchill, Captain Peter
    (Raoul) 9, 66–81, 88,
    90–4, 96–101, 103–11,
    113, 117–8, 120–2, 125,
    130, 142, 143, 146–8, 157,

161, 162, 166–8, 173, 176, 181–8, 192, 195, 204, 215, 219, 220, 224, 230

Churchill, Prime Minister Winston 9, 27, 35, 36, 108, 143, 239, 240–2, 244, 245

Clauberg, Carl 133

COMBAT network 73

Cottets, The 98, 103, 104, 193

Dachau 149, 245

Deladier 25, 26

Dunkirk 27, 239

Eisenhower, General 143, 175, 177

Franco, General 25

Frager, Paul 93–5, 98, 120, 218

Fresnes prison 9, 10, 102, 107, 110, 112, 118, 120, 122, 235

First Aid Nursing Yeomanry 46, 50, 151, 235

Gaulle, General Charles de 33, 37, 134, 135, 183, 216, 225

Girard 91, 92, 95, 97, 98, 100, 184

Göring, Hermann 151

Hallowes, Geoffrey 167–9, 231

Hellinger, Dr 167

Herail, Simone Marie Gabrielle 118

Hess, Rudolf 122, 151

Himmler, Heinrich 126, 131, 135, 136, 138

Hitler, Adolf 25–8, 33, 39, 114, 139, 141, 150–2, 245

invasion of Southern France 134

Ivy, Andrew 154

Jepson, Selwyn 38, 39, 45, 180, 194, 203, 227

Lefort, Cecily 136

London Charter 150

Macmillan, Prime Minister Harold 196–7

Markowicz, Dr 144–5

Marsac 65, 80, 81, 84, 95, 100–2, 106, 107, 118, 120–1, 123

Marseille 65, 66, 74, 80–7, 95, 100, 218, 235

medical experiments 126, 128, 137, 149, 155

Mewes, Margaret 131, 155

Montgomery, Field Marshal 63, 242

Mory, Carmen 155

Munich Conference 26

Mussolini 25, 242, 244

Neagle, Dame Anna 10, 163, 164
Nicholas, Elizabeth 170, 171, 190
Noble, George 89
Normandy 20, 21, 23, 132, 134, 243

Operation Clothier 59, 61–3, 65, 67, 69
Operation Sea Lion 28–9
Overton-Fuller, Jean 170–1, 190, 201

Pétain, Marshal 28, 33
Phoney War 26, 28
poliomyelitis 17, 19, 20, 167, 227
Prosper Circuit 172, 178

Rabinovitch, Captain (Arnaud) 78, 160, 218
Ramdohr, Ludwig 155
Raoul *see* Captain Peter Churchill
Ravensbrück 10, 123–4, 126–33, 135, 137–40, 142, 144–5, 148–9, 151–3, 155, 157, 159, 163, 167, 171, 179, 183, 193, 194, 198, 205, 228, 232
Rolfe, Lillian 136, 166, 233

Sachsenhausen 122, 146
St Jorioz 94, 98, 100, 101, 103, 104, 108, 219
Salvequart, Vera 153, 155
Sansom, Roy 23, 27, 29, 43, 146, 157
Schwartzhuber, Johann 155
Shidlausky, Gerhard 155
Spindle network 68, 70–1, 73, 75, 77, 79, 104
Suhren, Fritz 134–5, 138, 141, 142, 155, 167, 183, 194
Szabo, Violette 136, 162, 166, 167, 169, 221–3, 232

Treite, Percy 155
Truda 130

Uckermark 127

Versailles, Treaty of 24, 26
Vichy government 28, 33, 36, 72, 76–7, 83
Vichy, police 28, 72
von Skene, Eugenia 155

War Crimes Tribunals 9, 148–51, 155, 207, 221
Ward, Dame Irene 171, 179, 188, 190–3, 195–9, 214–6, 225, 227
Wilcox, Herbert 162–4

The History Press
The destination for history
www.thehistorypress.co.uk